Successful Library Displays

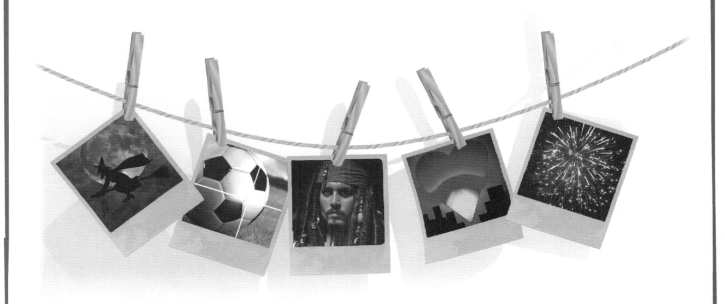

Fran Knight
Pat Pledger

CAREL PRESS

D1344342

Introduction

Welcome to Successful Library Displays.

This book is designed to help the busy librarian make the library a vibrant centre of learning. Using key dates in the calendar, you can show students the range of fiction and present your stock in new and dynamic ways.

Most pages have a brief introduction to the theme, display ideas, themed activities, further information and a reading list.

The themes
Chosen to take you right through the calendar year, the themes range from the serious (Refugee week, 3rd week in June) to the purely fun (Talk like a pirate day, 19th September) with many others coming somewhere between the two.

The themes offer an ideal opportunity to liaise with departments, for example Bastille Day with the French department, religious festivals with RE, Guy Fawkes with history. There are even opportunities for contact with the elusive maths and science departments.

Of course you may wish to use an idea at a different time from its particular 'day'. To help with this we have included an index on page 72.

Reading lists
No attempt has been made to label the reading age or level of the fiction in the reading lists. As we all know, what is suitable for one 14 year old will seem babyish to another and too mature for a third. The reading lists therefore cover a variety of ages. Those printed on the page will be a handy reference or reminder to help you to select from your stock. The lists are also supplied as Word documents (just email us to obtain them) so that you can easily print them and alter them to suit your library and your students. You could even produce them as posters or bookmarks.

For more guidance you could use Readplus - an online database of fiction organised under themes.
Visit **www.carelpress.com** to find out more.

Display ideas
We have assumed that you will always make a display of as many of the related books as are appropriate so this is generally not repeated in the text unless there is some particular reason to do so.

Many colleagues have sent photos of their displays which can be found here:
www.carelpress.co.uk/libraryresources/Displayphotos
We'd be very happy to receive more.

Further info
We assume that you and your students are aware of Wikipedia (not always 100% reliable, of course) so we have only referenced this on pages where the information is particularly useful or is the best source we have found.

We have visited all the websites that we have included to check that they are both relevant and current. You will find that many of them contain display ideas or educational resources.

Websites are also provided in Word documents to save you having to type them (please email us to obtain them).

Some general websites which may be of use are:

For quotes:
www.quotegarden.com

For flags of the world to colour
www.crwflags.com/fotw/flags/cbk.html

For outline maps
www.eduplace.com/ss/maps

The Carel Press resources Fact File and Essential Articles contain statistics and pieces of journalism relevant to the themes covered. To help you find them we have suggested a search term to use with the Quicksearch facility on our website.
www.carelpress.com/quicksearch
Whenever you see *QuickSearch:* you will have the ability to generate instantly a list of associated statistics and articles to use for background or development. In addition there are Fact File worksheets on our website which you can use with groups.

For associated organisations, use the thematic guide in Carel Press's Key Organisations

This edition © Fran Knight, Pat Pledger, Carel Press 2009

Editor: Christine A Shepherd

Advisor: Claire Larson

Additional ideas: Rosemary Broadbent, Manager, Leeds School Library Service

Designer: Jack W V Gregory

Cover Design: Anne Louise Kershaw

Published by Carel Press, 4 Hewson St, Carlisle CA2 5AU
Tel + 44 1228 538928
info@carelpress.com
www.carelpress.com

Printed by: Finemark, Poland

CIP Data: British Library Cataloguing in Publication Data is available

ISBN: 978-1-905600-18-2

Contents

Contents

Displays for any time .. ..Pages 61-69

General display ideas .. ..Pages 70-71

Index . .. . Page 72

Horses' Birthday

All thoroughbred horses are given the same official birthday. This is January 1st in the northern hemisphere but August 1st in the southern hemisphere to reflect the different foaling seasons.

Display

Borrow a saddle, reins, whip, boots and horse riding equipment to decorate the area around the spinner and the circulation desk.

Pin up posters of Black Beauty, Red Rum and any other famous horses.

Activities

Have a 'Name the horse' competition – horses are often named for their appearance or character. Race horses sometimes have names made up from their parents' names, for example Red Rum's sire was Quorum and his dam was Mared.

Show a film such as Black Beauty, Seabiscuit or Champions at lunchtime.

Invite a jockey, a stable owner or someone who works there to give a short talk. They may be able to lend some items for your display

Further info

Suggestions for names:
www.horses-and-horse-information.com/horsenames/a.shtml

www.funhorsenames.com

There are some excellent clips of the National Theatre's production of "War Horse" available on YouTube

For articles & statistics see Essential Articles & Fact File: carelpress.com/quicksearch
QuickSearch: Horse

Reading list - Happy birthday horse

Constable, Kate .. .. The taste of lightning

Daniel, Lucy. .. .. Shetland in the shed

Davidson, Leon . .. . Animal heroes

Evans, Nicholas .. .. The horse whisperer

Flanagan, John . .. . Erak's ransom

Forsyth, Kate.. .. .. The tower of ravens

Ghent, Natale . .. . No small thing

Hale, Shannon .. .. The goose girl

Hoffman, Alice .. .. The foretelling

Hoffman, Mary .. .. Stravaganza: City of stars

Ibbotson, Eva . .. . The star of Kazan

Jones, Diana Wynne.. .. .. .. The Pinhoe Egg

Lawrence, Caroline .. .. The charioteer of Delphi

Lewis, C. S... .. .. The horse and his boy

McCaughrean, Geraldine .. .. Cowboy Jess

Matthews, L.S. .. .. After the flood

Morgan, Michaela .. .. Night flight

Morpurgo, Michael . .. . Farm boy

Morpurgo, Michael . .. . War horse

O'Hara, Mary .. .. My friend Flicka

Peyton, K.M. .. .. Flambards

Peyton, K.M. .. .. Minna's quest

Philbrick, Rodman .. .. Fire pony

Roberts, Katherine . .. . I am the great horse

Sewell, Anna .. .. Black Beauty

Steinbeck, John .. .. The red pony

Thompson, Kate .. .. Annan water

HOLOCAUST
MEMORIAL DAY

The dictionary definition of holocaust is destruction or slaughter on a massive scale. The Holocaust usually refers to the murder of more than 6 million Jews by the Nazi regime during the Second World War. 27 January is the anniversary of the liberation of the Auschwitz-Birkenau death camp. Holocaust Memorial Day has been widened to include other groups and other genocides but there is some criticism that it ignores some groups and events.

The Holocaust Memorial Day website provides information, posters, logos, book group activities, film lists and eyewitness accounts as well as other resources.

Display

Make gigantic posters on the theme, *Stand up and be counted,* for display around the school and your library.

Make a super large cut-out of the logo for display.

Display a map of the world prominently showing the countries where holocaust and genocide have happened.

Make mock candles to have around the library and near your display of the books which tell of this horror.

Hana's suitcase by Karen Levine will make an incredible display idea. Use an old battered suitcase and set it up as in the book, at the bottom of the spinner. Add the markings found in the story, with some information about the book.

www.hanassuitcase.ca (shows a photo of Hana)

Further Info

www.hmd.org.uk

For outline maps
www.eduplace.com/ss/maps

For articles & statistics see Essential Articles & Fact File:
carelpress.com/quicksearch
QuickSearch: Prejudice

Reading list - Holocaust: Stand up and be counted

Al-Windawi, Thura .. .. Thura's diary

Boyne, John .. .. The boy in the striped pyjamas

Dickinson, Peter .. .. AK

Ellis, Deborah. .. .. Parvana

Ellis, Deborah. .. .. Parvana's journey

Ellis, Deborah. .. .. Shauzia

Filipovic, Zlata .. .. Zlata's diary

Frank, Anne. .. .. The diary of Anne Frank

Gleitzman, Morris .. .. Once

Gleitzman, Morris .. .. Then

Hicyilmaz, Gaye .. .. Smiling for strangers

Hoffman, Mary .. .. The colour of home

Jarman, Julia.. .. .. Hangman

Laird, Elizabeth . .. . Kiss the dust

Laird, Elizabeth . .. . A little piece of ground

Levi, Primo .. .. If this is a man

Mertus, Julie .. .. The suitcase: refugee voices from Bosnia and Croatia

Morpurgo, Michael . .. . The Mozart question

Pausewang, Gudrun.. .. .. .. Fall out

Pressler, Miriam .. .. Malka

Roy, Jennifer .. .. Yellow star

Toksvig, Sandi .. .. Hitler's Canary

Zephaniah, Benjamin .. .. .. Refugee boy

Zusak, Markus .. .. The book thief

Poverty & Homelessness Action Week

Poverty and Homelessness Action Week is timed to take place each year after Holocaust Memorial Day but before the beginning of Lent. It usually occurs in the 1st week of February and is extended to 8 days to take in 2 Saturdays.

Display

Set up a display with a moth-eaten sleeping bag (on an old park bench, if possible). Add some old blankets, newspaper, and some empty tins near a spinner containing books that have homeless characters in them.

Activities

Bin to collect food

Ideally in advance, organise some students to
- Collect stories from local or national newspapers
- Find out what is done for the homeless locally, what local churches are doing and how students can help.

See if you can find someone who volunteers – time or money – who will talk about this activity.

Further Info

www.housingjustice.org.uk

www.centrepoint.org.uk
Includes accounts of young homeless people

www.childhope.org.uk
Works with street children worldwide. Contains examples of their writing and art

www.shelter.org.uk
Contains accounts of young people in housing need

These websites have been chosen because they offer useful resources for your display. However, there are many other housing charities and organisations. For a fuller list please see the latest Key Organisations (Carel Press).

For articles & statistics see Essential Articles & Fact File: carelpress.com/quicksearch
QuickSearch: Poverty, homeless

Reading list - Give me shelter

Alvtegen, Karin . . .. Missing

Arrigan, Mary . . .. Hard luck

Ashley, Bernard. .. . . Angel boy

Burgess, Melvin .. . . Junk

Cushman, Karen.. . .. . The midwife's apprentice

Ellis, Deborah. .. . . Shauzia

Ellis, Deborah. .. . . Parvana's journey

Ellis, Deborah. .. . . Diego, run!

Ellis, Deborah. .. . . Diego's pride

Ellis, Deborah. .. . . Looking for X

Fox, Paula. .. . . Monkey Island

Gaiman, Neil .. . . Neverwhere

Grindley, Sally .. . . Broken glass

Jamet, Delphine .. . . Street kid in the city

Kelleher, Annette . . .. Pumpkin head is dead

Kennen, Ally .. . . Bedlam

Laird, Elizabeth . . .. The garbage king

McPhail, Catherine . . .. Missing

McPhail, Catherine . . .. Roxy's baby

Marchetta, Melina .. . . On the Jellicoe Road

Mistry, Rohinton .. . . A fine balance

Pausewang, Gudrun.. . .. . .. Fall out

Rapp, Adam .. . . 33 snowfish

Sachar, Louis . . .. Holes

Swindells, Robert .. . . No angels

Swindells, Robert .. . . Stone cold

Swindells, Robert .. . . Wrecked

Thebo, Mimi .. . . Hit the road, Jack

Trevor, William .. . . Felicia's journey

Waddell, Martin. .. . . Tango's baby

Marie Curie Cancer Care

World Cancer Day activities are part of a 5 year programme to prevent cancer by making good lifestyle choices.

Display

The daffodil is the symbol of Marie Curie Cancer Care which is engaged in both care and research. Make cut-outs and tissue paper daffodils to decorate the library. Instructions here: www.daffodilusa.org/references/tissuepaperdaffodils.html

Download the logos for the various cancer organisations and have a class make them into large posters or hangers or displays for the library.

Display information about famous cancer survivors – Kylie Minogue, Lance Armstrong – consider whether to include those who did not survive – Jade Goody.

Activities

MacMillan Cancer Support holds the world's biggest coffee morning every September. Why not hold an early version in the library? Get the students or student council to organise it.

Get students to research various cancer charities and make posters about the activities of each one. Decide (vote?) on one to support.

Read aloud, at lunchtime some of the picture books which deal with dying from cancer. These include Sadako.

Further Info

www.worldcancercampaign.org
Resources on this site include downloadable posters in English, French and Spanish

www.cancerresearchuk.org
Has downloadable resources

www.mariecurie.org.uk

www.macmillan.org.uk

www.teenagecancertrust.org
Contains accounts from young cancer sufferers, pictures of gigs for the charity and links to other useful sites

These websites have been chosen because they offer useful resources for your display. However, there are many other cancer charities and organisations. For a fuller list please see the latest Key Organisations (Carel Press).

For articles & statistics see Essential Articles & Fact File: carelpress.com/quicksearch
QuickSearch: Cancer

Reading list - Cancer is a word, not a sentence

Bauer, Joan . .. . Hope was here

Coerr, Eleanor .. .. Sadako and the thousand paper cranes

Dickens, Barry .. .. My grandfather

Downham, Jenny . .. . Before I die

Geras, Adele .. .. Silent snow, secret snow

Gleitzman, Morris .. .. Two weeks with the queen

Hannigan, Katherine . .. . Ida B

Hearn, Julie . .. . Follow me down

Higgins, Chris. .. .. 32C, that's me

Hoffman, Mary .. .. Stravaganza: City of masks

Kelleher, Damian. . .. . Life interrupted

Kuipers, Alice. .. .. Life on the refrigerator door

Le Vann, Kate. . .. . Things I know about love

McGowan, Anthony .. .. Henry tumour

Morgan, Nicola . .. . Fleshmarket

Morimoto, Junko . .. . My Hiroshima

Nicholls, Sally. .. .. Ways to live forever

Picoult, Jodi .. .. My sister's keeper

Rapp, Adam .. .. Under the wolf, under the dog

Segal, Erich . .. . Love story

Singleton, John. .. .. Skinny B, Skaz and me

Stone, Miriam. .. .. At the end of words, a daughter's memoir

Vercoe, Elizabeth . .. . Keep your hair on

Wild, Margaret .. .. Jinx

Wilson, Jacqueline . .. . Lola Rose

Valentine's Day   # 14th February

Valentine's Day is named for Saint Valentine. Little is known about the saint but his feast day has been associated with love since at least the middle ages.

Display

In the library, cut out large red, sparkly hearts and have them hanging over the display, by the displays, on the display, on the library doors.

Cut out smaller hearts and stick them into books.

Post pictures of 'romantic' authors around the school, these could include Barbara Cartland, Brontë Sisters, Jane Austen, Daphne Du Maurier, Cathy Hopkins and Jacqueline Wilson.

Activities

Give out heart shaped cut-outs with the names of romance books.

Around the school, place piles of 'Love is in your library' cards, to attract attention. Put heart shaped lists of books in staff pigeon holes to put up in the classrooms.

'Broken hearts' – Give out half a heart with a book name and get students to find the other half – the author's name – which would be hidden inside a book (and vice versa).

Further Info

Check out the following sites for information about the saint:

www.catholic.org/saints/saint.php?saint_id=159 (Catholic Online)

www.newadvent.org/cathen/15254a.htm

saints.sqpn.com/saint-valentine-of-rome/

For articles & statistics see Essential Articles & Fact File: carelpress.com/quicksearch
QuickSearch: Love, romance, marriage

Reading list - Love is in the air

Austen, Jane .. .. Pride and prejudice	**Ibbotson, Eva** . .. . The secret countess
Bennett, Veronica .. .. Angelmonster	**Klein, Lisa**. .. .. Ophelia
Blackman, Maloraie .. .. Checkmate	**Landman, Tanya** .. .. The goldsmith's daughter
Blackman, Malorie.. .. .. Knife edge	**Limb, Sue** . .. . Girl 16, pants on fire
Blackman, Malorie.. .. .. Noughts and crosses	**McCombie, Karen** .. .. My funny valentine
Brontë, Emily.. .. .. Wuthering Heights	**Meyer, Stephenie** . .. . Twilight
Brooks, Kevin. .. .. Candy	**Manning, Sarra** . .. . Guitar girl
Cann, Kate .. .. Possessing Rayne	**Marchetta, Melina** .. .. Saving Francesca
Cassidy, Cathy .. .. Scarlett	**Peyton, K.M.** .. .. Greater gains
Cohn, Rachel and Levithan, David . .. . Nick & Norah's infinite playlist	**Price, Susan** .. .. The Sterkarm handshake
Cohn, Rachel and Levithan, David . .. . Naomi and Ely's no kiss list	**Rees, Celia** .. .. Sovay
Clarke, Judith. .. .. One whole and perfect day	**Rai, Bali** . .. . (Un)arranged Marriage
Dhami, Narinder .. .. Bollywood babes	**Rennison, Louise**. .. .. Stop in the name of pants
Earls, Nick .. .. Monica Bloom	**Rosoff, Meg**. .. .. How I live now
Gardner, Sally. .. .. The red necklace	**Sacher, Louis** . .. . Small steps
Hartnett, Sonya. .. .. The ghost's child	**Sedgwick, Marcus**.. .. .. Blood red, snow white
Hearn, Lian.. .. .. Tales of the Otori (series)	**Smith, Dodie** .. .. I capture the castle
Heyer, Georgette.. .. .. Frederica	**Spinelli, Jerry** .. .. Love, Stargirl
Hoffman, Mary .. .. The falconer's knot	**Turnbull, Ann**.. .. .. No shame, no fear
Hooper, Mary.. .. .. By royal command	**Vaught, Susan** .. .. Big fat manifesto
Hopkins, Cathy . .. . Looking for a hero	**Westerfeld, Scott**. .. .. Pretties
	Wing, Rachael .. .. Love-Struck
	Wilson, Jacqueline . .. . Love lessons

20th February

Celebrated for the first time in 2009, this is a day set aside to promote equality and inclusion in all aspects of society.

Display

Take a chance with some gritty literature, by displaying some of the latest books written for teens that push the boundaries, and make the reader more aware of social injustice around the world. Use a sign saying Gritty Literature, Grit Lit or Get your teeth into these.
- Remind staff and students that some of these books will push the acceptable boundaries of children's reading.
- Display criticism of these books including some critical reviews.
- Have a piece of paper with the book title on it to allow students to write a comment as soon as they have read the book and to respond to the comments of others.

Display some books considered 'gritty' from the past or their parents' era.

Display books which dealt with social injustice in the past (Uncle Tom's cabin, Cry the beloved country, To kill a mockingbird etc.)

Display a poster of the declaration of human rights. carelpress.co.uk/posters

World Day of Social Justice

Activities

Make up a list of social justice issues such as poverty, exploitation, lack of legal representation, etc. Pin these words up with a list of books about that issue. Encourage the students to add their own reading.

Pin up photos which show Social Injustice (eg lack of water).

Cut out articles from newspapers and statistics of homeless children, children living in poverty or fear, child soldiers. Add to the display, and match to books.

Further Info

www.un.org/esa/socdev/social/intldays/IntlJustice/

www.un.org/millenniumgoals/

www.childhope.org.uk
Works with street children worldwide. Contains examples of their writing and art

www.hrw.org
Campaigning worldwide for human rights

For articles & statistics see Essential Articles & Fact File: carelpress.com/quicksearch
QuickSearch: Wider world, human rights

Reading list - Grit Lit

Adichie, Chimamanda Ngozi Half of a yellow sun	**Guevera, Ernesto.** .. .. The motorcycle diaries
Ashley, Bernard. .. .. Angel boy	**Hicyilmaz, Gaye** .. .. Pictures from the fire
Ashley, Bernard. .. .. Smokescreen	**Laird, Elizabeth** . .. . A little piece of ground
Beah, Ishmael .. .. A long way gone: memoirs of a boy soldier	**Laird, Elizabeth** . .. . Kiss the dust
Bell, Julia .. .. Dirty work (mature)	**Latifa** .. .. My forbidden face
Boyle, T Coraghessan .. .. The tortilla curtain	**Le Carre, John** .. .. The constant gardener
Brooks, Geraldine .. .. Nine parts of desire	**Le Carre, John** .. .. The mission song
Brooks, Geraldine .. .. People of the book	**McCormick, Patricia** .. .. Sold
Clinton, Cathryn .. .. A stone in my hand	**McGowan, Anthony** .. .. The knife that killed me
Dirie, Waris .. .. Desert children	**Muhsen, Zana** .. .. Sold: a story of modern day slavery
Dirie, Waris .. .. Desert dawn	**Nazer, Mende** . .. . Slave
Ellis, Deborah. .. .. Diego's pride	**Satrapi, Marjane** .. .. Persepolis
Ellis, Deborah. .. .. Parvana	**Seierstad, Asne.** .. .. The bookseller of Kabul
Ellis, Deborah. .. .. Parvana's journey	**Smith, Roland.** .. .. Peak
Ellis, Deborah. .. .. Diego, run!	**Stratton, Allan** .. .. Chanda's secrets
Ellis, Deborah. .. .. Shauzia	**Sunderland, Alan** . .. . Refugee: the diary of Ali Ismail
Ellis, Deborah. .. .. The heaven shop	**Suzuma, Tabitha** .. .. From where I stand
Fugard, Athol . .. . Tsotsi	**Swarup, Vikas** .. .. Q and A (Slumdog millionaire)
Gavron, Jeremy. .. .. Moon	**Swindells, Robert** .. .. Stone cold
Ghosh, Amitav .. .. The hungry tide	
Grindley, Sally .. .. Broken glass	

Eating Disorders Awareness Week   Last week in February

Obviously a sensitive subject, we've approached the display element as an opportunity to emphasise healthy eating. However, the reading list and websites approach the problem more directly.

Many of these ideas and activities would also be good for World Health Day on April 7th.

Display

Have posters of "5 a day" around the display. Many posters are available from greengrocers, markets or health advisory agencies.

Have fruit and vegetables hanging around. Make large cut outs of fruit and vegetables such as apples, cherries, oranges, potatoes, carrots etc. Hang them above the circulation desk, near the library entrance, near the display. Make them as big and colourful as possible.

Activities

Have a healthy lunch day in the library or have a share fruit and vegetable day.

There are many biographies and autobiographies about people who have suffered from eating disorders. Ask at your local library or your school library service.

Further Info

www.pbs.org/wgbh/nova/thin/ (Dying to be thin)

www.b-eat.co.uk
Resources include video from survivors and videos showing how images are manipulated

www.rcpsych.ac.uk/mentalhealthinfoforall/problems/eatingdisorders.aspx
Offers help and guidance leaflets as well as recommended reading on this and a number of mental health issues.

www.eatwell.gov.uk

www.food.gov.uk

www.5aday.nhs.uk

There are many video clips about eating disorders on the web – easily found via Google. It is obviously important to view them before showing the students.

For articles & statistics see Essential Articles & Fact File: carelpress.com/quicksearch
QuickSearch: Eating disorder

Reading list - Eat to live, not live to eat - Cicero

Antieau, Kim .. .. Mercy, unbound

Barham, Peter .. .. The invisible girl

Bell, Julia .. .. Massive

Best, Elizabeth .. .. Eli's wings

Bird, Carmel .. .. The Bluebird Cafe

Brill, Sarah .. .. Glory

Child, Lauren .. .. I will not ever never eat a tomato (picture book)

Dessen, Sarah .. .. Just listen

Fathallah, Judith .. .. Monkey taming

Fielding, Helen .. .. Bridget Jones's diary

Fine, Anne .. .. Charm school

Flinn, Alex .. .. Diva

Forde, Catherine .. .. Fat boy swim

Glover, Sandra .. .. Face to face

Going, K.L. .. .. Fat kid rules the world

Gottlieb, Lori .. .. Stick figure: a diary of my former self

Hautzig, Deborah. .. .. Second star to the right

Hutchings, Melinda. .. .. Fighting for life

Kaslik, Ibi .. .. Skinny

Levine, Gail Carson .. .. Fairest

Mackler, Carolyn .. .. The earth, my butt & other big round things

McLarty, Ron .. .. The memory of running

McNicoll, Sylvia. .. .. Walking a thin line

Menzie, Morgan .. .. Diary of an anorexic girl

Vaught, Susan .. .. Big fat manifesto

Vrettos, A.M. .. .. Skin

Welford, Sue .. .. Secrets

Wells, Rosemary, Brown, Marc ill. .. .. The Gulps (picture book)

Wilson, Jacqueline .. .. Clean break

Wilson, Jacqueline .. .. Girls under pressure

Saint David (Dewi Sant in Welsh) was a monk, living in the 6th century. He lived an austere life and expected the same from his followers.

Among the miracles associated with him are miraculous appearances of springs of water and a sudden upheaval of earth into a mound so that the congregation could see and hear him.

His advice to his followers was to "Do the little things" that would lead them to the right path.

St. David's Day in Wales is a celebration of culture, language and identity.

Display

Hang the national flag of Wales and the flag of St David.

Have the Welsh names for the saint and Wales in large poster form around the library as well as some common Welsh words.

Have daffodils and leeks in abundance.

Some classes may like to try their hand at making daffodils: **www.daffodilusa.org/references/tissuepaperdaffodils.html**

Display the words from Henry V Act 4 Scene 7, which talks about the Welsh archers with leeks in their headwear.

Activities

Some activities are available to copy: **www.dltk-kids.com/world/wales/index.htm** (flag, shield, dragon, leek soup recipe and worksheets)

Have pictures of dragons around the library. Find all the dragon books available and display them.

Have some Welsh choral music in the background for the day.

Further Info

For a Welsh flag to colour:
www.enchantedlearning.com/europe/wales/flag/flagquizbw.shtml

For background:
www.bbc.co.uk/wales/history/

For information about the flag of St David:
www.crwflags.com/FOTW/flags/gb-w-std.html

For lots of background information:
www.wales.com

For language:
www.bbc.co.uk/wales/learnwelsh/

As a starting point for learning about Welsh myths and legends:
home.freeuk.com/pjanderson/storiesfromwales/whoswho.html

Versions of the myths:
www.webmesh.co.uk/Mabinogionhomepage.htm

The story of Gelert:
www.beddgelerttourism.com/gelert/

Reading list - Y Ddraig Goch

Bawden, Nina . .. . Carrie's war

Cooper, Susan .. .. The grey king

Garner, Alan . .. . The owl service

Rees, Celia .. .. The wish house

Sutcliff, Rosemary .. .. The lantern bearers

Wilson, Jacqueline .. .. Buried alive

Wales is rich in myths and legends – such as those which inspired 'The Owl Service." Many of these are contained in Mabinogion. Students will probably respond to the story of Gelert "The faithful hound" whose grave at Beddgelert, North Wales, is a tourist attraction.

Crufts Dog Show

The first Crufts dog show took place in 1891. In 1958, a year after the death of the owner Charles Cruft, his widow sold the show to the Kennel Club, which runs it today – it is the largest dog show in the world. A controversy about the breeding and health of pedigree dogs led to the BBC cancelling its coverage and later to the Kennel Club revising some breed standards.

Display

Set up a display of your students' photos of their dogs. Ask them to bring a photo in – with their name and class marked clearly on the back. Sort out a safe area to display them eg foyer, wall, circulation desk. This could lead to a 'Best in Show' competition for your school.

Some students may have dog toys, fluffy dogs, dog leads, blankets etc that they would like to display.

Display photos of the variety of different breeds. Ask students to bring in photos of more exotic breeds to display.

Use a kennel or a dog basket with blanket and bowl to advertise the display in the foyer or the library.

Display doggy books like *Marley and me*, *Lassie*, and *The incredible journey* in a dog basket.

Hang a clutch of leads from the ceiling near the display.

Ask your local vet or pet shop if they would like to participate in the display, or set up their own, or lend you some posters for your display.

March (usually 1st or 2nd week)

Activities

Invite people in to show off their Guide Dogs and talk to the students.

Have a demonstration by the local dog handlers club or dog obedience school or army/police dog handler.

Pin up a range of dog names. (You could ask a class to make a poster or flash cards.) Students could do a survey of dog names used by the school population. Students might like to investigate some of the very fancy names given to show dogs – go to the results section of the Crufts website for examples.

Have a competition asking students to write or tell their favourite dog story. Staff could also contribute.

For Primary schools, read some doggy picture books to students at lunch time (bring tissues).

Further Info

www.crufts.org.uk (Official website of Crufts)

www.dogstrust.org.uk

www.petsastherapy.org

For information about breeds
www.thekennelclub.org.uk

For information about guide dogs
www.guidedogs.org.uk

For articles & statistics see Essential Articles & Fact File:
carelpress.com/quicksearch
QuickSearch: Dog

Reading list - Dog day afternoon

Abadzis, Nick . .. . Laika

Armstrong, William. .. .. Sounder

Burnford, Sheila .. .. The incredible journey

Cassidy, Cathy .. .. Lucky star

Cole, Babette . .. . Truelove (picture book)

Creech, Sharon. .. .. Love that dog

Dalkin, Philip .. .. Dogstar

De Bernieres, Louis .. .. Red dog

DiCamillo, Kate. .. .. Because of Winn-Dixie

Dodd, Lynley . .. . Hairy Maclary from Donalson's dairy (picture book)

Doder, Joshua .. .. A dog called Grk

Doyle, Roddy.. .. .. The giggler treatment

Doyle, Roddy.. .. .. Wilderness

Fine, Anne .. .. Care of Henry

French, Jackie .. .. Pete the sheep (picture book)

Graham, Bob.. .. .. The trouble with dogs

Grogan, John . .. . Marley, a dog like no other

Haddon, Mark .. .. The curious incident of the dog in the night-time

Hoopman, Kathy.. .. .. All dogs have ADHD

Johnson, Pete .. .. Ghost trouble

King-Smith, Dick.. .. .. Babe

London, Jack . .. . The call of the wild

London, Jack . .. . White Fang

Michael, Livi .. .. Sky wolves

Moon, Pat. .. .. Barking mad

Mooney, Bel .. .. Best dog Bonnie

Morpurgo, Michael. .. .. Best Mate

Ness, Patrick.. .. .. The knife of never letting go

Newberry, Linda .. .. Windfall

Paulsen, Gary. .. .. Ice race

Paulsen, Gary. .. .. My life in dog years

Pearce, Philippa .. .. A finder's magic

Priestley, Chris.. .. .. Dog magic!

Strong, Jeremy . .. . Where's that dog?

Strong, Jeremy . .. . The hundred mile an hour dog

1st Wednesday in March

Mathematics Day

Founded in 2007, the intention is to get all over the world participating in Maths games and setting world records.

Display

Numbers and shapes: Hang a series of large numbers and shapes from the ceiling or counter.

Highlight things with numbers on them: canisters, typewriters, word processors, kitchen scales, kitchen measuring jugs and spoons, newspapers, books, shoes, clothing, etc.

Arrange playing cards in a fan shape across the top of the spinner or attach to a coat hanger.

Display clothes in ascending order of size.

Hang up some recipe books, atlases, street directories, logarithm books, slide rules, rulers, tape measures, different sizes of screwdrivers, set squares etc.

Activities

Show *Good Will Hunting* at lunch time.

Have a series of measuring cups, or spoons or jugs near the circulation desk for students to examine. Put measuring tape on the ground from one area in the library to another, ask students to pace it out, then measure it. Have a tin of dice for students to play with at lunchtime. Set up a chess set.

How would we live without Maths? Take a recipe, remove the values and quantities and see how easy students think it would be to follow. You could do the same for directions and instructions.

Marvel at the mathematical ability of autistic children. Read aloud sections from Mark Haddon's *The curious incident of the dog in the night time.*

Display some maps and set up Google Earth so that students can use grid references to find key places, the school, shops, cinema or even their homes.

For Primary Schools: display picture books, The Very Hungry Caterpillar by Eric Carle, One bear at bedtime by Mick Inkpen for example.

Further Info

www.worldmathday.com

For articles & statistics see Essential Articles & Fact File: carelpress.com/quicksearch
QuickSearch: Maths

Reading list - More numbers than you can count

Adams, Douglas .. .. The hitchhiker's guide to the galaxy

Anno, Masaichiro. .. .. Anno's mysterious multiplying jar

Asimov, Isaac. .. .. Foundation

Baldacci, David. .. .. Simple genius

Brown, Dan.. .. .. Digital fortress

Brown, Dan.. .. .. The Da Vinci Code

Buchan, John. .. .. The thirty-nine steps

Choldenko, Gennifer . .. . Al Capone does my shirts

Crichton, Michael .. .. Jurassic Park

Deary, Terry. .. .. The lion's slave

Doctorow, Cory .. .. Little brother

Eco, Umberto. .. .. The name of the rose

Egan, Greg .. .. Schild's ladder

Enzensberger, Hans Magnus The number devil : a mathematical adventure

Galvin, Ray .. .. Fibonacci's cows (picture book)

Gibson, William. .. .. The difference engine

Green, John. .. .. An abundance of Katherines

Guedj, Denis .. .. The parrot's theorem

Haddon, Mark .. .. The curious incident of the dog in the night-time

Harris, Robert .. .. Engima

Herbert, Frank .. .. Children of Dune

Huxley, Aldous .. .. Brave new world

Inkpen, Mick .. .. One bear at bedtime (picture book)

Juster, Norton .. .. The phantom tollbooth

King, Laurie R. .. .. The beekeeper's apprentice

Lalwani, Nikita .. .. Gifted

L'Engle, Madeline .. .. A wrinkle in time

Larbalestier, Justine.. .. .. .. Magic lessons

Larbalestier, Justine.. .. .. .. Magic or madness

Larbalestier, Justine.. .. .. .. Magic's child

Le Guin, Ursula K. .. .. The dispossessed

Mitton, Tony .. .. Spookyrumpus

Nasar, Sylvia .. .. A beautiful mind

Neville, Katherine .. .. The eight

Pappas, Theoni. .. .. The adventures of Penrose: the mathematical cat

Pears, Iain .. .. An instance of the fingerpost

Robinson, Kim Stanley. .. .. The years of rice and salt

Scieszka, Jon .. .. Maths curse (picture book)

Swift, Jonathan. .. .. Gulliver's Travels

Tolstoy, Leo. .. .. War and peace

Wells, H. G.. .. .. The time machine

Westerfeld, Scott. .. .. The secret hour

Westerfeld, Scott. .. .. Touching darkness

Westerfeld, Scott. .. .. Blue noon

World Book Day

A celebration of books and reading.

Display

Display a selection of books written by authors around the world and display a map of the world with links to the books.

Check the newspaper and display all the information you can find in it regarding international authors.

Ask publishers and book shops for brochures and flyers about international authors and books.

List some of the authors in your local area, highlighting those from overseas.

Activities

What was the first book your students read? Ask them to bring in their first book to put in the display. Staff may like to be involved as well. Make sure every book is labelled, and protected during the day.

What are your parents' favourite books? Ask the parents of students to lend their favourite book for a display. Again be vigilant about caring for someone else's book.

Which book changed your life? Ask students and staff to display a book that changed their way of thinking, their pathway through life, or their thoughts on some major issue. Make a pro forma for them to use, so that your display can be standardised. The pro forma may include

1st Thursday in March

who the person is, a little about them, the book they have chosen and why. Why not involve your book group and invite entries from the wider community too, such as the Mayor, local sports people or local retailers. The list is endless!

A good starting point might be Camden Library's list of 100 books that shaped the last century.
www.camden.lib.nj.us/kids/books.htm

Further Info

www.worldbookday.com
Go to the website above and register your school to receive promotional material that can be used in your display. Quick Reads, part of the World Book Day, aims to get people who have had difficulty with reading in the past, to read. Check out the link from World Book Day to get promotional material and hints to use in the library.

The Big Read: Global Action for Literacy: UNESCO's World Book and Copyright day is on 23rd April.
portal.unesco.org

The Global Campaign for Education: The Big Read:
www.campaignforeducation.org/bigread
www.sendmyfriend.org

For outline maps:
www.eduplace.com/ss/maps

For articles & statistics see Essential Articles & Fact File:
carelpress.com/quicksearch
QuickSearch: Reading

Reading list - People die, but books live on

Austen, Jane .. .. Northanger Abbey	**Jones, Lloyd** .. .. Mister Pip
Bradbury, Ray .. .. Fahrenheit 451	**Keioskie, Luke** .. .. Room one nineteen
Chabon, Michael.. .. .. Wonder boys	**King, Stephen** .. .. Misery
Colfer, Eoin . .. . The legend of Spud Murphy	**Krauss, Nicole** .. .. The history of love
Connolly, John .. .. The book of lost things	**Le Guin, Ursula K.** .. .. Powers
Cunningham, Michael .. .. The hours	**Le Guin, Ursula K.** .. .. Voices
Edwards, Kim. .. .. The memory keeper's daughter	**McEwan, Ian** .. .. Atonement
Fforde, Jasper .. .. The Eyre affair	**Nafasi, Azar** .. .. Reading Lolita in Tehran
Fforde, Jasper .. .. Lost in a good book	**Philbrick, Rodman** .. .. The last book in the universe
Fforde, Jasper .. .. The well of lost plots	**Ruiz Zafon, Carlos** . .. . The shadow of the wind
Fine, Anne .. .. Bad dreams	**Schlink, Bernhard** .. .. The reader
Fowler, Karen Joy .. .. The Jane Austen book club	**Sedgwick, Marcus**.. .. .. Blood red, snow white
Funke, Cornelia .. .. Inkheart	**Setterfield, Diane** .. .. The thirteenth tale
Gray, Keith .. .. The chain	**Skelton, Matthew.** .. .. Endymion Spring
Hardinge, Frances . .. . Fly by night	**Winchester, Simon**.. .. .. The surgeon of Crowthorne
Harris, Robert .. .. The ghost	**Zusak, Markus** . .. . The book thief

March 2nd week   National Science and Engineering Week

National Science and Engineering Week (NSEW) is a ten day celebration of science, engineering and technology. The website includes an archive of past events. The list of events shows science in a huge variety of contexts.

See below for a separate section on Astronomy.

Display

Display all the science fiction books you can find.
Display novels with a science theme (see list).
Promote the Science section in Dewey.
Borrow some animals, such as rats, or lizards, from your Science Lab.

Display old mechanical things, cameras, typewriter, computer, washing machine, scrubbing board, TV, wireless, cooking implements, old bicycle, or anything which has changed markedly over the years.

If you can, add old medical equipment, as well as some medical books from second hand bookshops or some empty bottles of medicine. Search out an old medicine cabinet and put Cod Liver Oil etc in it.

Activities

Show The Hitchhiker's Guide to the Galaxy at lunchtime Eoin Colfer has been commissioned to write a further 'Hitchhiker' entitled 'And another thing', this sequel is scheduled to be published on 12/10/09. Information about the project can be found on his website:
eoincolfer.com

Have a Science Fiction readathon.
There are some wonderful 'science fiction' novels, which show society as it may be in the near future. They include:
- The declaration and The resistance by Gemma Malley
- Unwind by Neal Shusterman
- The other side of the island by Allegra Goodman

All show a nasty future with elements of today. Why not display a spinner full of these novels, with some classics from the past like 1984, A brave new world, A clockwork orange and Animal farm? These novels are classed as Dystopian fiction (see list in general section).

Encourage your students to write a piece of speculative fiction to show what the future may hold.

Ask students to draw up a future vision of the school premises.

What about a library of the future? Ask students to design a library for 2030 when they will be adults.

Further Info

www.britishscienceassociation.org

For articles & statistics see Essential Articles & Fact File:
carelpress.com/quicksearch
QuickSearch: Science

Astronomy

2009 was designated as the International Year of Astronomy, the activities and evaluation continue into 2010 and their impact is expected to last much longer.
www.astronomy2009.org

Display

Have a space theme around the book display.

Flexible ducting material is wonderful for making space ships, space suits, space worms or space aliens to put around your display. Pin up some astronomy posters. Have a galaxy of planets and stars hanging from the ceiling. Stick stars on the ceiling, or hang stars from the spinner, with names of novels on each star.

Have large silver stars leading the students into the library.

Hang lots of long, curly silver strips from the ceiling above your display.

Display information about Galileo, Kepler, Copernicus and others.

Find large images of the moon and some of the planets to hang. (See RAS site in 'Activities')

Create a display with stars, the planets, aliens and space ships.

Display some of the Sci Fi classics by Jules Verne, H. G. Wells, Philip Dick, Aldous Huxley, Arthur C Clarke, Ursula le Guin etc.

Activities

Show Apollo 13 at lunchtime.

A booklist of science fiction stories with good astronomy and physics is at
www.astrosociety.org/education/resources/scifi.html
Some of these may be available in second hand shops and would be of interest to avid science students.

For other resources select the education section of the Royal Astronomical Society
www.ras.org.uk

hubblesite.org

For those who would like to be able to identify the stars they see, the young stargazers section of the Society for Popular Astronomy is very helpful.
www.popastro.com

Reading list - Science - 'an imaginative adventure of the mind'
Sir Cyril Herman Hinshelwood

Anderson, Laurie Halse .. .. .. Catalyst

Anderson, M.T... .. .. Astonishing life of
Octavian Nothing

Anderson, M.T... .. .. Feed

Asquith, Ros .. .. Girl writer: spies and lies

Atwood, Margaret .. .. Oryx and Crake

Bear, Greg .. .. Blood music

Beckett, Bernard . .. . Genesis

Blackman, Malorie.. .. .. Operation Gadgetman!

Buckley-Archer, Linda.. .. .. .. Gideon the cutpurse

Burgess, Melvin .. .. Bloodtide

Burgess, Melvin .. .. Bloodsong

Carmody, Isobelle .. .. A fox called Sorrow

Corder, Zizou.. .. .. Lionboy: The truth

Corder, Zizou.. .. .. Lionboy: The chase

Craig, Joe. .. .. Jimmy Coates: Killer

Craig, Joe. .. .. Jimmy Coates: Target

Dickinson, Peter .. .. Eva

Farmer, Nancy .. .. The house of the scorpion

Fox, Helen .. .. Eager

Fox, Helen .. .. Eager's nephew

Heath, Jack . .. . The Lab

Higson, Charlie . .. . Silverfin

Horowitz, Anthony.. .. .. Scorpia

Mark, Jan.. .. .. The electric telepath

McAuley, Paul J. .. .. White devils

Malley, Gemma . .. . The declaration

Malley, Gemma . .. . The resistance

Mark, Jan.. .. .. The electric telepath

Mowll, Joshua .. .. Operation Red Jericho

Oppel, Kenneth. .. .. Skybreaker

Patterson, James .. .. The angel experiment

Pearson, Mary .. .. The adoration of Jenna
Fox

Pfeffer, Susan Beth. .. .. Life as we knew it

Pratchett, Terry . .. . Nation

Reeve, Philip .. .. Larklight

Robinson, Kim Stanley. .. .. .. Sixty days and counting

Shearer, Alex .. .. The speed of the dark

Thompson, Kate .. .. The fourth horseman

Wells, H. G... .. .. The island of Dr. Moreau

Westerfeld, Scott. .. .. Peeps

Westerfeld, Scott. .. .. Specials

Reading list - Look to the stars

Andy Griffiths . .. . Zombie Bums from
Uranus

Fienberg, Anna.. .. .. Borrowed light

Haldeman, Joe.. .. .. The forever war

Horowitz, Anthony.. .. .. Ark angel

Jones, Diana Wynne.. .. .. .. Dogsbody

Niven, Larry . .. . Ringworld

Nix, Garth .. .. Grim Tuesday

Paterson, Katherine .. .. The same stuff as stars

Pratchett, Terry . .. . The last hero

Pratchett, Terry . .. . Nation

Reeve, Philip .. .. Larklight

Reeve, Philip .. .. Mothstorm

Reeve, Philip .. .. Starcross

Robinson, Kim .. .. Red Mars

8th March

International Women's Day

Founded in 1911, this is a day to celebrate women's achievements. Each year a different global theme is set but local groups also focus on their own particular issues.

Display

Purple, green and white were the colours of the suffragette movement which campaigned for votes for women.

Tie purple, green and white ribbons all over the display and circulation desk.

Have all staff wear these colours.

Display purple and green vegetables, linen, crockery, bookmarks, books, flowers etc.

Display as many books by women authors as you can: crime books, picture books, women illustrators. Classic women authors such as the Brontës, Mrs Gaskell, Daphne du Maurier and Agatha Christie.

Feature women from a variety of careers such as scientists, researchers, managing directors etc. You can often pick up articles about successful women from newspapers and magazines. Try to feature local women too.

Display clothing from the past:
Womens' uniforms (nursing, armed forces, shopkeepers, nuns etc), costumes from past eras, underwear, shoes, and hats make good displays.
Compare the school uniform for girls now and in the past. Find some pinafores and aprons to display. Ask your school population to bring in aprons. (Make sure they are labelled.)

Domestic equipment. Display some old cooking equipment, scrubbing board, scrubbing brush, sandsoap, old iron, sweeper, etc.

Activities

At lunch time read aloud picture books by women.

Invite one or two local women from the community in to talk to the students.

Further Info

www.internationalwomensday.com

For articles & statistics see Essential Articles & Fact File:
carelpress.com/quicksearch
QuickSearch: Women

Reading list - Go get 'em girls

Bray, Libba .. .. Far sweet thing

Carter, Ally .. .. I'd tell you I love you, but then I'd have to kill you

Cashore, Kristin .. .. Graceling

Castellucci, Cecil. .. .. Beige

Clayton, Sally Pomme .. .. .. Amazons! Women warriors of the world

Clare, Cassandra. .. .. City of bones

Colfer, Eoin.. .. .. The wish list

Darke, Marjorie. .. .. A question of courage

Enthoven, Sam.. .. .. The black tattoo

Fforde, Jasper .. .. The Eyre affair (and sequels)

Forsyth, Kate.. .. .. The tower of ravens (Rhiannon's ride series)

Gaiman, Neil .. .. Coraline

Golding, Julia. .. .. The diamond of Drury Lane

Goodman, Alison. .. .. The two pearls of wisdom

Grindley, Sally .. .. Spilled water

Howell, Simmone. .. .. Notes from the teenage underground

Ihimaera, Witi. .. .. Whale rider

Landman, Tanya .. .. Apache

Landman, Tanya .. .. The goldsmith's daughter

Larson, Kirby.. .. .. Hattie Big Sky

Levine, Gail Carson .. .. Ella enchanted

Lott, Tim .. .. Fearless

McCaughrean, Geraldine .. .. The white darkness

McKinley, Robin .. .. The blue sword

McKinley, Robin .. .. The hero and the crown

Mahy, Margaret. .. .. The magician of Hoad

Marchetta, Melina .. .. On the Jellicoe Road

Miller, Kirsten. .. .. Kiki Strike: Inside the shadow city

Murdock, Catherine Gilbert .. Dairy queen

Murdock, Catherine Gilbert .. Princess Ben

Newbery, Linda. .. .. Polly's march

Nix, Garth .. .. Sabriel (and sequels)

Patterson, James .. .. The angel experiment

Pierce, Tamora.. .. .. Alanna: the first adventure (and sequels)

Pratchett, Terry. .. .. Nation

Pullman, Philip .. .. Northern lights

Pullman. Philip .. .. The Ruby in the smoke

Riordan, James. .. .. War song

Storr, Catherine. .. .. Marianne dreams

Trease, Geoffrey .. .. Bring out the banners

Westerfeld, Scott. .. .. Uglies (and sequels)

Wilson, Jacqueline .. .. The dare game

St Patrick's Day

Everyone can be Irish for a day! Or at least celebrate all things Irish.

Display

Display posters of Ireland – particularly ancient monuments and gaelic crosses.

Display the Irish flag.

Put shamrocks around the book display.

Activities

Have the staff wear green clothes.

Have a staff morning tea with green food or Irish food.

Display the story of St Patrick in episodes round the library - make it a library pilgrimage.

Further Info

For a very full account of life of St. Patrick:
www.newadvent.org/cathen/11554a.htm

Easier and less detailed:
www.catholic.org/saints/saint.php?saint_id=89

US site with video:
www.history.com/content/stpatricksday

For customs and traditions including leprachauns:
www.marvelicious.com/stpatrick.html

For traditions recipes and jokes:
www.theholidayspot.com/patrick

For flags to colour:
www.crwflags.com/fotw/flags/cbk.html

Reading list - Have a shamrocking day

Barry, Sebastian	The secret scripture
Binchy, Maeve	Circle of friends
Cassidy, Cathy	Scarlett
Ciddor, Anna	Night of the fifth moon
Colfer, Eoin	Airman
Colfer, Eoin	The legend of Captain Crow's teeth
Conlon-McKenna, Marita	Wildflower girl
Conlon-McKenna, Marita	The fields of home
Conlon-McKenna, Marita	Under the hawthorn tree
Dowd, Siobhan	Bog child
Dowd, Siobhan	A swift pure cry
Doyle, Roddy	Paddy Clarke ha ha ha
Drinkwater, Carol	The hunger: the diary of Phyllis McCormack, Ireland 1845-1847
Gibbons, Alan	The defender
Hyland, M.J.	Carry me down
Lawhead, Stephen	Patrick: son of Ireland
Lingard, Joan	The twelfth day of July
Lisson, Deborah	Red Hugh
Lutzeier, Elizabeth	Crying for the enemy

McCourt, Frank	Angela's ashes
Marillier, Juliet	Child of the prophesy
Marillier, Juliet	Son of the shadows
Mehran, Marsha	Pomegranate soup
Morpurgo, Michael	The ghost of Grania O'Malley
Morpurgo, Michael	Twist of gold
Napoli, Donna Jo	Hush: an Irish princess' tale
O'Brien, Edna	Down by the river
Pilling, Ann	Black harvest
Sansom, Ian	Mr Dixon disappears
Sansom, Ian	The case of the missing books
Sefton, Catherine	Shadows on the lake
Sefton, Catherine	Starry night
Thompson, Kate	Creature of the night
Thompson, Kate	The last of the high kings
Thompson, Kate	The new policeman
Thompson, Kate	The fourth horseman
Toibin, Colm	The heather blazing

21st March

World Poetry Day

The day designated by UNESCO to promote the reading, writing, publishing and teaching of poetry.

Display

Display some favourite poems.

Display verse novels (see list).

Display a list of recent laureates with examples of their poetry.
A list of poets laureate and their dates of 'service' can be found here:
www.poetsgraves.co.uk/poets_laureate%20uk.htm

Display poetry books (too numerous and varied to list) especially humorous ones.

The Kiss

Over a bag of fish and chips,
He said he loved me.
That moment I've treasured from that day to this
The taste of salt in that living kiss.

Tracy Rayner (student)

This poster is part of the Posters for English series from Carel Press.

Activities

Encourage students to write a short story in a verse novel format.

Display first lines of some poems and ask students to find the poem.

Have a poetry competition. Publish students' poems in the school newsletter.

Any books by Sandy Brownjohn, such as "Does it have rhyme?", will provide a host of poetry related activities.

Some 'story' poems lend themselves to being retold in picture book form, for example OUP's 1999 edition of *The Highwayman* illustrated by Charles Keeping. Display any that you have and invite students to nominate other poems for this treatment. They could illustrate one verse or one section of a poem.

Further Info

www.poetrysociety.org.uk

www.love-poems.me.uk

www.poetrylibrary.org.uk

www.poetryuk.com

www.poets.org

Times article on how to become a poet
entertainment.timesonline.co.uk/tol/arts_and_entertainment/books/poetry/article6068997.ece

www.warpoetry.co.uk

Reading list - Poetry is plucking at the heartstrings
(Dennis Gabor)

Blackman, Malorie .. .. Cloud busting

Brown, Susan Taylor.. .. .. .. Hugging the rock

Creech, Sharon . .. . Heartbeat

Creech, Sharon . .. . Love that dog

Levithan, David . .. . The realm of possibility

McCormick, Patricia.. .. .. .. Sold

Rosen, Michael . .. . Even more nonsense

Roy, Jennifer .. .. Yellow star

Sones, Sonya . .. . What my mother doesn't know

Wild, Margaret .. .. Jinx

Wild, Margaret .. .. One night

Wolff, Virginia Euwer . .. . True believer

Wolff, Virginia Euwer . .. . Make lemonade

International Day for the Elimination of Racial Discrimination

21st March is the anniversary of the day in 1960, when police opened fire and killed 69 people at a peaceful demonstration in Sharpeville, South Africa. They were demonstrating against the "pass laws" – part of the Apartheid system which discriminated against all non-white South Africans. These laws meant that black people had to carry a pass to prove they had permission to be in 'white' areas.

Display

Display hard hitting images of the results of racism such as concentration camps, Jewish humiliation, wearing of arm bands, civil war, segregation, apartheid, persecution of certain groups such as gypsies, homosexuals etc.

Further Info

www.un.org/depts/dhl/racial/

Anne Frank Trust UK
www.annefrank.org.uk

Football's anti-racism campaign: Kick It Out
www.kickitout.org

Martin Luther King Center
www.thekingcenter.org

The Equality and Human Rights Commission
www.equalityhumanrights.com

For articles & statistics see Essential Articles & Fact File:
carelpress.com/quicksearch
QuickSearch: Race

Reading list - Racism - No way!

Abdel-Fattah, Randa	Ten Things I Hate About Me
Adlington, L.J.	The diary of Pelly-D
Alexie, Sherman	The absolutely true diary of a part-time Indian
Anderson, M.T.	The pox party
Ashley, Bernard.	Rapid
Ashworth, Sherry.	Close-up
Birch, Beverley.	Rift
Blackman, Malorie.	Knife edge
Blackman, Malorie.	Noughts and crosses
Boyle, T. Coraghessan	The tortilla curtain
Boyne, John	The boy in the striped pyjamas
Breslin, Theresa	Divided city
Brown, Eric.	British Front
Childs, Rob.	Black and white
D' Aguiar, Fred	The longest memory
De Mari, Silvana	The last elf
Forde, Catherine.	Skarrs
Gavin, Jamila.	Grandpa's Indian summer
Gavron, Jeremy.	Moon
Gibbons, Alan.	Caught in the crossfire

Glass, Linzi	The year the gypsies came
Glass, Linzi	Ruby Red
Greder, Armin.	The island
Hesse, Karen.	Witness
Hicyilmaz, Gaye	Girl in red
Hicyilmaz, Gaye	Pictures from the fire
Johnson, Pete	The hero game
Landman, Tanya	Apache
McKee, David,	Tusk, tusk (picture book)
MacPhail, Catherine	Under the skin
Martin, S. I.	Jupiter Williams
Naidoo, Beverley	The other side of truth
Paulsen, Gary.	Nightjohn
Paulsen, Gary.	Sarny, a life remembered
Rai, Bali	The last taboo
Rai, Bali	What's your problem?
Riordan, James.	Rebel cargo
Rodman, Mary Ann.	Yankee girl
Spinelli, Jerry	Maniac Magee
Taylor, Mildred	Roll of thunder, hear my cry
Teo, Hsu-Ming	Behind the moon

World Water Day is an International Day to make people aware of the fragility of our most precious resource.

Display

Find a small windmill or small rainwater tank as a focus for the display and include hoses and buckets etc. Include both plants that need a great deal of watering and those that need very little.

Put up posters of water being used around the world.

Display any of the huge amounts of information published daily in newspapers.

Which countries have problems with water? Put up a world map and pinpoint those countries where water is a major problem (eg South East Australia's rainfall has reduced by half).

Activities

Set up some experiments with the science staff.

Have a Save Water Day: Measure the amount of water wasted in the school or the library. Measure the capacity of a rainwater tank. How will it save water for the school?

Find out:
• What your local council is doing to save water.
• What the government is doing to conserve water.
• About the water restrictions around the world.

Design a poster to reinforce water conservation.

Do a survey on what families are doing to conserve water at home.

Further Info

www.worldwaterday.org
(There is a different theme each year.)

Water Aid UK: **www.wateraid.org/uk/**

For outline maps:
www.eduplace.com/ss/maps/

See The Atlas of Water available from Carel Press.

For articles & statistics see Essential Articles & Fact File: carelpress.com/quicksearch
QuickSearch: Water

Reading list - Every drop counts

Bertagna, Julie .. .. Exodus

Dickinson, Peter .. .. Water

Ghosh, Amitav .. .. The hungry tide

Gleitzman, Morris .. .. Belly flop

Gleitzman, Morris .. .. Water wings

Grindley, Sally .. .. Spilled water

Hale, Shannon .. .. River secrets

Hamilton, Margaret H2O

Harris, Robert .. .. Pompeii

Herbert, Frank .. .. Dune

Jarrar, Nada Awar .. .. Dreams of water

McCaughrean, Geraldine .. .. Not the end of the world

Mark, Jan .. .. Useful idiots

Meyer, Kai .. .. The water mirror (series)

Nicholson, William .. .. Firesong

Stewart, Paul & Riddell, Chris .. .. Midnight over Sanctaphrax

Twain, Mark .. .. The adventures of Huckleberry Finn

April Fools' Day

The origins of April Fools' Day are ancient but unclear. The tradition of playing tricks on people seems to have evolved at the same time in several countries but with local variations.

Display

Make up a spaghetti tree (as in the BBC hoax).

Display all the funny books you can find (see book list). You could also display joke and cartoon books.

Have a mannequin dressed as a fool or jester. Or pin a jester's costume up to the display board.

Post a list of all the names used for the fool: jester, harlequin, clown, puppet etc.

Find pictures of all the different fools, and display them. Include the joker from playing cards and from Batman.

Activities

Set up a joke board for students to write up a joke and display it or make a joke tree, hanging kids' jokes from the branches. Have a joke blog, but be prepared to vet this for unsuitable content.

Have a competition/vote for the best joke.

Encourage students to make April Fools' Day cards. Find a book that explains how to make pop-up cards or use the following website and try some at lunchtime **www. robertsabuda.com/popmakesimple.asp**

Read aloud some of Andy Griffiths jokes and short poems. Have students write their own poems.

Read Roald Dahl's stories, eg Matilda, at lunchtime.

Read Roald Dahl's fairy tales and ask students to make up something similar.

Get students to research the role of the fool in Shakespeare's plays and the role of the fool in court.

Make some jesters' hats at lunchtime with students, some instructions can be found here: **play.powerhousemuseum.com/makedo/jesters_hat.php**

Further Info

en.wikipedia.org/wiki/April_Fools_Day

www.museumofhoaxes.com/hoax/aprilfool/

www.alexthejester.com/html/historyPopup.html (History of the jester)

Reading list - Laugh a minute

Almond, David .. .. .My dad's a birdman	**Hopkins, Cathy** . .. . .Zodiac girls: recipe for rebellion
Cabot, Meg.. .. .. .How to be popular	**Kennen, Ally** .. .. .Berserk
Colfer, Eoin.. .. .. .Artemis Fowl	**Landy, Derek** .. .. .Skulduggery Pleasant
...and the eternity code	**Landy, Derek** .. .. .Skulduggery Pleasant: Playing with fire
...and the Arctic incident	**Limb, Sue** . .. . .Girl 15, charming but insane
...the graphic novel	**Place, Nick** .. .. .The OK team
Colfer, Eoin.. .. .. .The supernaturalist	**Pratchett, Terry** . .. . .A hat full of sky
Colfer, Eoin.. .. .. .The wish list	**Rennison, Louise** . .. .. .Angus, thongs and full-frontal snogging
Deary, Terry . .. . .The fire thief	**Rees, Gwyneth**.. .. .. .The mum detective
Earls, Nick .. .. .Joel and Cat set the story straight	**Reeve, Philip** .. .. .Starcross
Elton, Ben. .. .. .Gridlock	**Riordan, Rick** . .. . .Percy Jackson and the Titan's curse
Fine, Anne .. .. .Ivan the Terrible	**Rosen, Michael** . .. . .Even more nonsense
Gaiman, Neil .. .. .Anansi boys	**Sacher, Louis** . .. . .Small steps
Gleitzman, Morris .. .. .. .Doubting Thomas	**Snicket, Lemony**.. .. .. .. .A series of unfortunate events
Gleitzman, Morris .. .. .. .Bumface	**Stanton, Andy** .. .. .Mr Gum Books
Gleitzman, Morris .. .. .. .Toad away	**Strong, Jeremy** . .. . .Beware! killer tomatoes
Gleitzman, Morris .. .. .. .Toad heaven	**Strong, Jeremy** . .. . .The hundred-mile-an-hour dog
Gleitzman, Morris .. .. .. .Toad rage	**Walliams, David** .. .. .The boy in the dress
Green, John. .. .. .An abundance of Katherines	**Wilson, Jacqueline** . .. .. .Girls in love
Griffiths, Andy .. .. .Zombie bums from Uranus	**Wolfer, Dianna** .. .. .The kid whose mum kept possums in her bra
Griffiths, Andy .. .. .The day my bum went psycho	**Wright, Rachel** .. .. .You've got blackmail
Griffiths, Andy .. .. .Bumageddon	
Griffiths, Andy .. .. .The cat on the mat is flat	
Griffiths, Andy .. .. .What bumosaur is that?	
Hopkins, Cathy . .. . .Mates, dates & cosmic kisses	

23rd April

The true date of Shakespeare's birthday is not known, but since he was baptised on 26th April, the 23rd has been traditionally used as his birthdate. It is also the date of his death.

Display

Put up happy birthday banners and balloons.

Display the various pictures of Shakespeare and have them as the outside edge of the display board with information about some of his best-known plays.

Use black and white cardboard to represent the black and white timbering of houses in his time; put your display over the top or between the half timbers.

Set up a small stage on which the books can be placed.

Photocopy front covers of the plays, placing them next to a book that is based on that play, eg cover of *Exposure* by Mal Peet next to *Othello* or *Ophelia* by Lisa Klein next to *Hamlet.*

Activities

Copy out Shakespeare quotes now popularly used, with a sign "Did you know these sayings are from the 16th century?" Quotes can be found in any Shakespearian handbook or Quotation book or look at **www.enotes.com/shakespeare-quotes/** You could also challenge students and staff to find which play they are from.

Shakespeare's Birthday

Have a video of one of his plays or one of the tie-ins to show at lunchtime. For example: *Shakespeare in love* or *Ten things I hate about you*.

Further Info

The Shakespeare Birthplace Trust has information about his life and the town where he grew up. **www.shakespeare.org.uk**

For easy access to plots and themes **www.shakespeare-online.com**

For fully annotated texts: **internetshakespeare.uvic.ca/index.html**

For a wide variety of resources and links **shakespeare.palomar.edu/**

For fun:

www.renfaire.com/Language/insults.html this generates Shakespearean insults

www.rinkworks.com/bookaminute/ for ridiculously shortened versions

Reading list - To be or not to be...

Blackwood, Gary L. .. .. The Shakespeare stealer

Broach, Elise .. .. Shakespeare's secret

Calder, Charlotte .. .. Cupid painted blind

Cooper, Susan .. .. King of Shadows

Deary, Terry . .. . The lord of the dreaming Globe

Early, Margaret . .. . Most excellent and lamentable tragedy of Romeo and Juliet

Fiedler, Lisa . .. . Dating Hamlet

Greenberg, Nicki .. .. Hamlet

Harris, Robert J. . .. . Will Shakespeare and the pirate's fire

Klein, Lisa . .. . Ophelia

Lacey, Josh . .. . Bearkeeper

Manning, Sarra . .. . Pretty things

Mark, Jan .. .. Heathrow nights

Mark, Jan .. .. Stratford boys

Marsden, John .. .. Hamlet

Peet, Mal .. .. Exposure

Pullman, Philip .. .. The butterfly tattoo

Rogers, Gregory .. .. The boy, the bear, the baron, the bard

Rogers, Gregory .. .. Midsummer Knight

Rosen, Michael . .. . What's so special about Shakespeare?

Schmidt, Gary D .. .. The Wednesday wars

Tiffany, Grace .. .. Ariel

Williams, Marcia .. .. Bravo, Mr. William Shakespeare!

St George's Day

St George is the patron saint of England but also of many other places including Ethiopia, Greece, Palestine, Portugal, and Russia. He is also the patron saint of many organisations including scouting. April 23rd is said to be the day he was martyred for refusing to give up his Christian faith.

Although he did exist as a historical figure, it is the legend of his slaying the dragon that is most famous.

Display

Hang an English flag over your display. Place other symbols of England around the library: roses, the three lions emblem as used by national sports teams, oak leaves.

Display items related to knights – armour, swords, lances, shields (all fake versions, of course), brass rubbings of tombs.

Display a large map of England.

Display the poem "Not my best side" by U A Fanthorpe together with a copy of the Ucello picture which inspired it. It tells the legend of St George from the point of view of the dragon, the princess and the knight in modern tones which are amusing and thought provoking. **www.english.emory.edu/classes/paintings&poems/uccello.html**

Display the story of the Wars of the Roses, with lots of red and white roses **www.warsoftheroses.com**

Display the speech from Henry V
shakespeare.mit.edu/henryv/henryv.3.1.html
Cry 'God for Harry, England and St. George.'

Activities

Show *Monty Python and the Holy Grail* at lunchtime.

Have a Medieval Day and invite some Morris Dancers or Mummers.

Find some picture books with St George to read at lunchtime.

Turn things on their head by reading *The paper bag princess* by Robert Munsch at lunchtime.

Further Info

For background:
www.britannia.com/history/stgeorge.html
saints.sqpn.com/saint-george/
faculty.smu.edu/bwheeler/Ency/St_George.html
www.ucc.ie/milmart/George.html (rather academic)

For the legend:
www.kellscraft.com/stgeorge.html
pages.videotron.com/chimere/contes/st-georges.html (in French)

As the patron saint of scouting:
pinetreeweb.com/stgeorge.htm

For flags to colour
www.crwflags.com/fotw/flags/cbk.html

For articles & statistics see Essential Articles & Fact File: carelpress.com/quicksearch
QuickSearch: Britain, England

Reading list - Let there be dragons

Bloor, Thomas .. .. Worm in the blood	Lansdown, Andrew. .. .. With my knife
Bradman, Tony.. .. .. Tom's dragon trouble	McCaffrey, Anne .. .. Dragonflight
De Mari, Silvana .. .. The last elf	McKinley, Robin .. .. The hero and the crown
D'Lacey, Chris .. .. Fire star	McKinley, Robin .. .. Dragonhaven
Funke, Cornelia. .. .. Dragon rider	Morpurgo, Michael .. .. Beowulf
George, Jessica Day . .. . Dragonskin slippers	Novik, Naomi.. .. .. His Majesty's dragon
Goodman, Alison . .. . The two pearls of wisdom	Paolini, Christopher .. .. Eragon
Hinds, Gareth . .. . Beowulf	Ridley, Philip .. .. Krindlekrax
Hobb, Robin .. .. Ship of destiny	Wilkinson, Carole. .. .. Dragonkeeper
Jordan, Sherryl . .. . The raging quiet	Wrede, Patricia C. .. .. Talking to dragons
Kiernan, Caitlin, Gaiman, Neil and Avary, Roger .. .. .. Beowulf	Yolen, Jane.. .. .. Dragon's blood

Freedom of the press is something we generally take for granted but in many parts of the world it is under attack. This is a day to celebrate and defend a free media.

Display

Display the books which are about the media (see reading list).

Put up copies of articles about the same story or topic from different newspapers.

Follow one story for the week, adding each day's articles.

The following website tells us about the number of people around the world who do not have freedom of the press. Highlight this information in your library. **www.wpfc.org/Challenges.html**

Activities

Check out stories of censorship, restriction and government newspapers in other countries.

Follow the story of the Watergate Affair. Show the film *Frost Nixon*.

Look at the Olympic Games in China and how the press was restricted there in 2008.

Invite a journalist in to talk about his/her freedoms.

Talk to the local newspapers about their policies regarding publishing sensitive material.

Watch the TV news/newspapers for censored material, eg pictures of people coming out of court with their faces obscured in some way. Ask questions about this form of censorship. Why is it allowed, why is it done?

Further Info

www.wpfc.org

Campaign for press and broadcasting freedom: **www.cpbf.org.uk**

For information on China and Olympics reporting restrictions: Human Rights Watch: **www.hrw.org**

For articles & statistics see Essential Articles & Fact File: carelpress.com/quicksearch

QuickSearch: Free speech or media (for a wider view)

Reading list - Celebrate your freedom to read uncensored material

All of these titles are set in the newspaper or TV business

Anderson, M.T... .. .. Feed

Ashley, Bernard. .. .. Down to the wire

Ashley, Bernard. .. .. Ten days to zero

Barr, Lollie .. .. The mag hags

Blacker, Terence .. .. Parent swap

Cassidy, Anne .. .. Looking for JJ

Child, Lauren.. .. .. Clarice Bean spells trouble

Flanagan, Richard .. .. The unknown terrorist

Fleischman, Paul . .. . Dateline: Troy

Gleitzman, Morris .. .. Bumface

Johnson, Pete .. .. I'd rather be famous

Kostakis, William . .. . Loathing Lola

Marks, Graham . .. . Omega Place: going underground

Marriott, Janice. .. .. The refugees

Oswald, Debra .. .. The fifth quest

Pullman, Philip .. .. I was a rat

Sedgwick, Marcus.. .. .. Blood red, snow white

Shearer, Alex . .. . Bootleg

Stewart, Paul . .. . Hugo Pepper

Vaught, Susan .. .. Big fat manifesto

White, Andrea .. .. Surviving Antarctica: reality TV 2083

International Day of Families

Visit the website below to check out the current theme.
www.un.org/esa/socdev/family/IDF.html

Display

On large pieces of cardboard make a long list of words which denote families (father, mother, sister, brother, sibling, parent, gran, grandma, aunt, uncle nephew, niece etc) and hang them above the display. You could have these lists in many languages and add pictures of different types of families from across the world. Have a range of families, one child family, two parent family, single parent family, grandparent family, lesbian family, siblings, no children, etc.

Have families of animals, families of objects, families of books.

Set up a family scene with TV, easychair, coffee table etc.

Have a different theme spinner (Fathers and Families, Mixed Families, Overseas Families, Families of Children).

Promote classics about families (Little Women, Anne of Green Gables, Little House on the Prairie).

Display Erica S. Perl's article below about families surviving hard times, as a parallel to what is happening today. Her article links to a slideshow of books and film clipswww.slate.com/id/2201710/

Further Info

Department for Children, Schools and Families website: www.dcsf.gov.uk

Famillies Worldwide website: www.fww.org

For articles & statistics see Essential Articles & Fact File: carelpress.com/quicksearch
QuickSearch: Family

Reading list - Families are forever

Bechard, Margaret . .. . Hanging on to Max

Birdsall, Jeanne .. .. The Penderwicks

Boyce, Frank Cottrell .. .. .. Millions

Clarke, Judith. .. .. One whole and perfect day

Colfer, Eoin.. .. .. Benny & Omar

Creech, Sharon. .. .. Chasing redbird

Dahl, Roald.. .. .. Danny, the champion of the world

Dhami, Narinder .. .. Superstar Babes

Doherty, Berlie .. .. Abela: the girl who saw lions

Doherty, Berlie .. .. Granny was a buffer girl

Dowell, Frances O'Roark .. .. Where I'd like to be

Ellis, Deborah. .. .. Diego, run!

Ellis, Deborah. .. .. Parvana (trilogy)

Fine, Anne .. .. Ivan the Terrible

Fine, Anne .. .. The Granny Project

Hartnett, Sonya. .. .. Surrender

Hendry, Diana. .. .. You can't kiss it better

Kennen, Ally .. .. Beast

Laird, Elizabeth . .. . Paradise end

Laird, Elizabeth. .. .. Red sky in the morning

Laird, Elizabeth. .. .. The Garbage King

Levithan, David . .. . Are we there yet?

McCaughrean, Geraldine .. .. Peter Pan in scarlet

Murdock, Catherine Gilbert .. Dairy queen

Murdock, Catherine Gilbert .. The off season

Napoli, Donna de . .. . Bound

Newbery, Linda . .. . Nevermore

Oldham, June. .. .. Smoke trail

Rai, Bali . .. . (Un)arranged Marriage

Rees, Gwyneth.. .. .. The mum detective

Rees, Gwyneth.. .. .. The mum hunt

Richardson, Nigel .. .. The rope ladder

Stevens, Leonie .. .. Eat well and stay out of jail

Weeks, Sarah . .. . So B. it

Wilson, Jacqueline . .. . Cookie

Wilson, Jacqueline . .. . The Diamond girls

Wilson, Jacqueline . .. . Starring Tracy Beaker

Wilson, Leslie. .. .. Last train from Kummersdorf

Wynne-Jones, Tim.. .. .. A thief in the house of memory

3rd week in May

Display

Fill the library with flowers.

Display all the flower pictures that you can and have your display board covered with flowers, or edged with flowers.

Set up a local map with horticultural attractions marked on it (gardens, council parks, heritage buildings, castles etc).

Pin up every piece of news you can find about the Flower Show near a display with books about gardening, or novels that have gardens in them. There are lots of picture books, for example Eric Carle's *The very hungry caterpillar*.

Activities

Invite students to set up a floral display. Encourage them to bring in flowers and plants for the week. Perhaps have a competition for the most colourful or unusual flower, plant, pot plant etc.

Make some flowers with your students, this site has some ideas and instructions:
www.howstuffworks.com/paper-flowers.htm
Make leis, floral garlands, floral headbands, floral bracelets.

Invite a florist in to talk to your students about floristry and making an attractive bouquet. Invite in some local gardeners to talk to classes.

Chelsea Flower Show

Invite the school community to wear a flower in their buttonhole for the week.

Further Info

www.rhs.org.uk/chelsea
Click onto Learning on the Chelsea Flower Show home page. This will take you to some of its publications, as well as information about school gardens. Your school may like to register and be part of the blooming of school gardens. The School Gardens section also contains information for teachers, recipes and hints.

Other major horticultural projects:

The Eden project
www.edenproject.com

The National Trust conserves some of the most spectacular gardens in the country
www.nationaltrust.org.uk

Royal Botanic gardens Kew
www.kew.org

For outline maps:
www.eduplace.com/ss/maps

Reading list - Bloomin' books

Ahlberg, Allan. .. .. The snail house

Anderson, Jodi Lynn. .. .. Peaches

Anholt, Laurence . .. . The magical garden of Claude Monet

Bjork, Christina .. .. Linnea in Monet's garden

Burnett, Frances Hodgson .. The secret garden

Dahl, Roald. .. .. James and the giant peach

Dickinson, Peter .. .. Tulku

Fleischman, Paul . .. . Weslandia

Foreman, Michael .. .. Mia's story

Garland, Sarah .. .. Eddie's garden and how to make things grow

Hoeye, Michael . .. . Time to smell the roses

Hoffman, Alice .. .. Green angel

Hoffman, Mary .. .. Stravaganza: City of flowers

Hooper, Mary. .. .. Petals in the ashes

Keyes, Daniel . .. . Flowers for Algernon

Pearce, Philippa .. .. Tom's midnight garden

Pierce, Tamora .. .. The magic in the weaving

Successful Library Displays   Carel Press www.carelpress.com

Display

Beg, borrow or steal some flags, bunting, posters of the final teams, or all the teams playing in the league to have around your library. Ask a class to be responsible for the setting up of the library before the big weekend.

Display all the football books.

Display potted biographies of the players.

Display information about other football competitions around the world (Australian Rules, Rugby, Gaelic Football, American Gridiron etc). Have a list of interesting facts about football displayed.

Display some magazines that feature articles about players, and show how much space is devoted to these sportspeople and their families.

Display some of the paraphernalia associated with football (boots, balls, shirts, timetables etc).

Create a display about women's football (see website links under further info). Feature your local team.

Activities

Ask a group of students to make a replica of the FA Cup.

Have a knitting competition to see who can make a scarf for the Final. Ask people to donate balls of wool for your students to make scarves.

Host a football quiz in the library at lunchtime. When did it start? Who is this year's champion? How many teams are involved? etc.

Encourage students to find out how much the players earn? (Write this up in large letters!). Cut out and display many of the advertisements that feature players.

Further Info

www.thefa.com
(Official website of the FA Cup)

en.wikipedia.org/wiki/FA_Cup

www.fifa.com

www.football-league.co.uk

Women's football:
www.thefa.com/Womens
womensfootball.eu/blog

For articles & statistics see Essential Articles & Fact File:
carelpress.com/quicksearch
QuickSearch: Football

Reading list - Kick that ball

Ahlberg, Allan.	The boyhood of Burglar Bill
Arksey, Neil	Playing on the edge
Ashley, Bernard.	Down to the wire
Blacker, Terence	The transfer
Blacker, Terence	On the wing
Browne, Anthony	Willy the wizard
Childs, Rob.	Black and white
Coleman, Michael	England
Dhami, Narinder	Bend it like Beckham
Durant, Alan	Doing the double
Durant, Alan	K O Kings
Durant, Alan	Barmy Army
Durant, Alan	Leagues apart
Durant, Alan	Kicking off
Durant, Alan	Stat man goes Greek
Foreman, Michael	War game
Freedman, Dan	The kick off
Gogerly, Liz	Footballers (non fiction)
Hornby, Hugh	Football (non fiction)
Jefferies, Cindy	Long shot (Stadium School series)
Jones, V.M.	Shooting the moon
Klass, David	Home of the braves
Laird, Elizabeth	A little piece of ground
Lynch, Chris	Inexcusable
McGowan, Anthony	The Bare bum gang and the football face-off
Morgan, Micaela	Respect
Morpurgo, Michael	Billy the kid
Palmer, Tom	Foul play
Peet, Mal	The penalty
Peet, Mal	Keeper
Rai, Bali	Dream on
Riordan, James.	When the guns fall silent
Riordan, James.	Match of death
Rosen, Michael	Even Stevens
Shearer, Alex	The great switcheroonie
Spurdens, Dave.	A new team is born: (Bridgewood High FC series)
Waddell, Martin.	Cup final kid
Wilson, Jacqueline	The dare game

June

Many students are fervently interested in the environment. Here the idea of recycling is being applied to books and to ideas.

Display

Have a spinner full of old favourites – from students or staff. Use your computer system to check which books are most often borrowed. Display the list with some of the books.

Display all the favourite classic stories you can find in your library (Jane Austen, Charles Dickens, Agatha Christie, Robert Louis Stevenson, Louisa May Alcott, Henry James, Jules Verne, Victor Hugo etc.)

Recycling is more than books, however, so why not display some books about recycling – ask your local council for information that you can display.

Display origami books. Encourage the students to make objects using recycled paper.

Are all stories just recycled plots? Check out the Seven Basic Plots: Rags to riches, quest, voyage and return, comedy, tragedy, rebirth, overcoming the monster. www.timesonline.co.uk/tol/news/uk/article1069369.ece
Have these displayed in your library. Ask students to add the title and author of the book they think fits the plot.

Recycled Plots. Display examples of stories being reworked in different ways, especially in film versions: *Romeo and Juliet* into *West Side Story* (and numerous other versions), *Pride and Prejudice* into *Bride and Prejudice* and *Emma* into *Clueless*.

Activities

Recycle some old books, or some classics, or some golden oldies. Have a book recycle day in your library, where students bring in a book they have read and no longer want and can swap it with another student.

Some people leave books near park benches or at bus shelters, train stations, etc so that people will read them see. www.bookcrossing.com

Have a book selling day or a book fair of secondhand books or promote the sale of old stock from the library.

Hold a Repair Your Favourite Book Day. See if someone in your community knows how to repair books properly, with glue, binding tape and muslin. Invite them in to hold a book repair day. Let the community know, and have them book in small groups for a workshop.

Brian Dettmer carves into books revealing the artwork inside, creating complex layered three-dimensional sculptures. centripetalnotion.com/2007/09/13/13:26:26/
Can anyone replicate this with old library books?

Have a competition in the school for the oldest book in the students' homes. Ask parents and grandparents to share their oldest books.

Introduce your students to Freecycle: www.freecycle.org – which is a bit like ebay but without any money.

Have a competition for the best use of something that has been thrown away.

Further Info

www.recyclenowpartners.org.uk

www.recyclenow.com

www.wrap.org.up

For articles & statistics see Essential Articles & Fact File: carelpress.com/quicksearch
QuickSearch: Recycle or environment (for a wider view)

Reading list - It's not junk!

Some picture books encourage recycling (not many novels, though). Display some of the picture books if you have them or borrow them from a junior school library to display.

Bethel, Ellie . .. . Michael Recycle	Hurst, Elise .. .. Misha's treehouse (young novel)
Burnside, Deborah . .. . This book is a load of rubbish (picture book)	Jeffers, Oliver. .. .. The great paper caper (picture book)
Gliori, Debi .. .. The trouble with dragons	McDonald, Megan .. .. Judy Moody saves the world
Hurst, Bridget. .. .. Look after your planet (characters created by Lauren Child)	Thaxton, Giles .. .. Spud goes green

World Environment Day

5th June

Established in 1972, this is one of the principal ways the United Nations stimulates worldwide awareness of the environment and promotes political action.

Display

On a spinner, have a different theme each day, such as endangered animals, environments, what people are doing to the environment, carbon emissions, greenhouse gases etc. Hang large branches above the spinner.

The UN website gives a World Environment Alphabet with hundreds of ways of doing something for the environment. Many of these can be adapted to a small or large display in your library. Examples include:

> Calculate your carbon footprint. Have footprints around the library to ask students to think about what impact they are having.

> Put up some alternatives to plastic bags.

> Promote bicycling. Securely hang a bicycle from the roof.

Make an equation to hang above the circulation desk or display, showing how trees offset carbon emission. To calculate your carbon footprint visit: **www.carbonfootprint.com/calculator.aspx**

Hang a poster showing what carbon trading is all about.

Display brochures about Solar Energy, Solar Hot Water, Recycled Water, Wind Turbines etc.

Activities

Promote Trees for Life.
www.treesforlife.org

Bring in some tubes with small trees and promote tree planting.

Further Info

www.unep.org
(United Nations Environment Program)

www.unep.org/wed
(World Environment Day website)

For information and free trees for schools
www.treeforall.org.uk

This commercial site has a handy animation to explain carbon offsetting.
www.jpmorganclimatecare.com/climate/how-offsets-help/animation/

This Guardian article explains the principles in a Q&A format **www.guardian.co.uk/environment/2007/jan/18/theissuesexplained.climatechange**

This site also offers to plant trees to offset carbon emissions - for a fee you can 'plant' trees online **www.sponsortrees.com**

This government website has information and resources on renewable energy **www.berr.gov.uk/energy/sources/renewables/schools/index.html**

For articles & statistics see Essential Articles & Fact File: carelpress.com/quicksearch
QuickSearch: Environment

Reading list - Save the Earth

Brooks, Martha . . . . Mistik Lake

Foreman, Michael . . . . One world

Hawke, Steve . . . . Barefoot kids

Hesse, Karen . . . . Out of the dust

Hiaasen, Carl . . . . Hoot

Hiaasen, Carl . . . . Flush

Hopkins, Cathy . . . . Mates, dates & saving the planet

James, Simon . . . . Dear Greenpeace

Lynch, Jim . . . . The highest tide

Mark, Jan . . . . Voyager

Mark, Jan . . . . Riding Tycho

Murdock, Catherine Gilbert . . Dairy queen

Murdock, Catherine Gilbert . . The off season

Oppel, Kenneth . . . . Airborn

Orr, Wendy . . . . Nim's island

Orr, Wendy . . . . Nim at sea

Paulsen, Gary . . . . Hatchet

Rosoff, Meg . . . . What I was

Smith, Roland . . . . Peak

Westerfeld, Scott . . . . Specials

Founded to celebrate our connection to the ocean and our dependence on it - and to help us protect it in future.

Display

Great fun would be had hanging cellophane strips from the ceiling to simulate seaweed, cutting out fish to hang as well, hanging shells on strings, cutting out large marine animals like sharks and whales, or decorating the library door with cellophane to welcome students to the sea cave.

Step out the dimensions of a Blue Whale in the library to give people an idea of its size. As it can be up to 33 metres long you may need to use a corridor! Wikipedia has a useful size comparison to a human. en.wikipedia.org/wiki/Blue_whale

Display a sailor's uniform.

Borrow someone's boat and display it filled with fishy and nautical books.

Set up part of the library like a jetty, display some oars, a sail, a shipping flag, fishing rods and lines, hooks and sinkers, fishing nets and buoys, lures and markers. Hang cut-outs of marine birds from the ceiling.

Have a coastal aquarium, with a rock pool environment with rocks, seaweed, crabs, limpets etc. Ask if any of the school population is interested in putting up a display of their aquaria.

Find some pictures from environmental organisations that show animals in the sea at risk from pollution. You may find some here: **www.greenpeace.org.uk/oceans**

Post some poems about the sea. See: **http://www.julianstockwin.com/Poetry.htm**

Decorate the circulation desk with fish cut-outs and find/make a treasure chest to decorate with seaweed, shells, skulls and spade. Fill it with books.

Display model ships.

Check out the local charity shop for fish knives and forks, fish moulds, old crockery with fish to display.

Activities

Show *Pirates of the Caribbean*, *Titanic* or *The Poseidon Adventure* at lunchtime.

Hold an early morning tea party for staff, serving things that are 'fishy'.

Further Info

www.theoceanproject.org/wod/
Marine Conservation Society: **www.mcsuk.org**

For articles & statistics see Essential Articles & Fact File: carelpress.com/quicksearch
QuickSearch: Ocean

Reading list - Sail away

Arnott, Susan . . . . The Astrolabe	**McKenzie, Anna** . . . . The sea-wreck stranger
Bateman, Colin . . . . Titanic 2020	**Mahy, Margaret** . . . . The riddle of the frozen phantom
Bowler, Tim . . . . Apocalypse	**Mark, Jan** . . . . Riding Tycho
Breslin, Theresa . . . . Saskia's journey	**Mark, Jan** . . . . Voyager
Brooks, Kevin . . . . Lucas	**Melville, Herman** . . . . Moby Dick
Colfer, Eoin . . . . Airman	**Molloy, Michael** . . . . Peter Raven, under fire
Cooper, Susan . . . . Greenwitch	**Morpurgo, Michael** . . . . Alone on a wide wide sea
Cooper, Susan . . . . Victory	**Morpurgo, Michael** . . . . Dolphin boy
Crowley, Bridget . . . . Ship's angel	**O'Brian, Patrick** . . . . Master and commander
Defoe, Daniel . . . . Robinson Crusoe	**Orr, Wendy** . . . . Nim's island
Dickinson, Peter . . . . The gift boat	**Philbrick, Rodman** . . . . The lobster boy
Dogar, Sharon . . . . Waves	**Philbrick, Rodman** . . . . The young man and the sea
Dowswell, Paul . . . . Battle fleet: Trafalgar 1805	**Potts, Stephen** . . . . Compass Murphy
Edwards, Christine . . . . . . On board the Boussole	**Pow, Tom** . . . . Captives
Forester, C.S. . . . . Captain Horatio Hornblower	**Pratchett, Terry** . . . . Nation
Hemingway, Ernest . . . . . . The old man and the sea	**Ransome, Arthur** . . . . We didn't mean to go to sea
Higson, Charlie . . . . Bloodfever	**Ridden, Brian** . . . . Sweet tea
Lee, Tanith . . . . Piratica	**Shearer, Alex** . . . . Sea legs
Lee, Tanith . . . . Piratica II Return to Parrot Island	**Snicket, Lemony** . . . . The grim grotto
Lynch, Jim . . . . The highest tide	**Rees, Celia** . . . . The cunning man
McAllister, Angela . . . . The tide turner	**Taylor, Theodore** . . . . Ice drift
	Wouk, Herman . . . . The 'Caine' mutiny

World Day to Combat Desertification and Drought

This covers the advance of deserts but is more concerned with the degradation of land by human activity, such as the removal of tree and plant cover.

Display

Display pictures of deserts around the world.

Find pictures of new deserts eg Aral Sea.

Have a sand tray and display books on wire frames.

Display some cactus plants.

Display statistics from this website:
www.didyouknow.cd/deserts.htm
Each year 30,000 square kilometers of land are swallowed up by deserts.
This results in more wildfire and storms, which erode and change the soil.
70% of land is affected by desertification.

Show pictures of dust storms. Show sand dunes encroaching upon cities/crops/towns/villages etc.

Download maps that show the increase in deserts.
Pin up a map of the world with the major deserts highlighted.
On the map of the world highlight those places where desertification is taking place.

Display any of the range of articles in the press about the struggling rivers of the world. On a map of the world, mark on the great river systems. Highlight those that are in trouble, particularly through man-made activities.

Further Info

www.unccd.int/publicinfo/june17/2009/menu.php

Scientific articles on desertification
www.sciencedaily.com/releases/2007/06/070619180431.htm

For simpler explanations, plus facts and figures
www.oxfam.org.uk/coolplanet/ontheline/explore/nature/deserts/facts.htm

www.geography.learnontheinternet.co.uk/topics/desert.html

For a description and photographs of the Aral sea:
oceanworld.tamu.edu/resources/environment-book/dyingseas.html

For articles & statistics see Essential Articles & Fact File:
carelpress.com/quicksearch
QuickSearch: Drought, Water (for a wider look)

Reading list - As dry as a bone

3rd week in June

Refugee Week is celebrated in the third week of June, usually between 15-21 June. It coincides with World Refugee Day on June 20. It aims to celebrate the contribution of refugees to the UK, and to encourage a better understanding between communities.

Display

Have some statistics available for kids to read. Basic facts are available at www.unhcr.org/basics.html

Display a map of the world with pointers showing the various places where refugees are. A class could take responsibility for this. They could find out where refugee camps exist and where war is causing refugees to flee. They could collect information from the newspapers or the internet, and use the map as a basis to show where these refugees are.

Set up a knapsack or back-pack, and ask students to think what is most important to them. Imagine they can only take a back-pack when leaving home for good. What would they take? Set up a tent and campfire, sleeping bag, and a small handful of belongings near your display.

Refugee Week

The United Nations website (www.unhcr.org) has a multitude of information about refugees. This is one of their big issues.

It is said that there are 67 million refugees in the world today; 6 million of these are Afghanis.

Show what 67 million looks like in your library. Have 67 pot plants, balls, books etc, showing that each represents 1 million people who are refugees. Have 67 pieces of paper on the wall, each with 1 million written on it.

Further Info

www.refugeeweek.org.uk

irr.org.uk/statistics/refugees.html

www.refugeestories.org

For outline maps:
www.eduplace.com/ss/maps

For articles & statistics see Essential Articles & Fact File: carelpress.com/quicksearch
QuickSearch: Refugees

Reading list - Walk in my shoes

Al-Windawi, Thura .. .. Thura's Diary

Anderson, Rachel .. .. Red moon

Ashley, Bernard. .. .. Freedom flight

Beames, Margaret.. .. .. Josef's bear

Bertagna, Julie.. .. .. Exodus

Breslin, Theresa .. .. Divided city

Chabon, Michael . .. . The final solution

Cornwell, Nicki.. .. .. Christophe's story

De Mari, Silvana .. .. The last elf

Ellis, Deborah. .. .. Parvana

Ellis, Deborah. .. .. Parvana's Journey

Ellis, Deborah. .. .. Shauzia

Gibbons, Alan. .. .. The dark beneath

Gleitzman, Morris .. .. Boy overboard

Gleitzman, Morris .. .. Girl underground

Gleitzman, Morris .. .. Once

Greder, Armin. .. .. The island

Hicyilmaz, Gaye .. .. Pictures from the fire

Hicyilmaz, Gaye .. .. Smiling for strangers

Ho, Minfong. .. .. The stone goddess

Hoffman, Mary .. .. The colour of home (picture book)

Honey, Elizabeth.. .. .. To the boy in Berlin

Jansen, Hanna .. .. Over a thousand hills I walk with you

Laird, Elizabeth. .. .. A little piece of ground

Laird, Elizabeth. .. .. Kiss the dust

Lasky, Kathryn .. .. Broken song

McCaughrean, Geraldine .. .. Not the end of the world

MacPhail, Catherine.. .. .. .. Under the skin

Morgan, Michaela .. .. Night flight

Morpurgo, Micheal . .. . The amazing story of Adolphus Tips

Naidoo, Beverley . .. . The other side of truth

Naidoo, Beverley . .. . Web of lies

Pausewang, Gudrun.. .. .. .. Fall out

Pressler, Mirjam .. .. Malka

Satrapi, Marjane .. .. Persepolis

Serraillier, Ian . .. . The silver sword

Shulevitz, Uri.. .. .. Map of dreams

Staples, Suzanne Fisher . .. .. Under the persimmon tree

Swindells, Robert .. .. Ruby Tanya

Tan, Shaun .. .. The arrival

Wilson, Leslie .. .. Last train from Kummersdorf

Wright, Denis.. .. .. Violence 101

Zephaniah, Benjamin .. .. .. Refugee boy

Zusak, Markus .. .. The book thief

American Independence Day 4th July

On 4th July 1776, 13 British colonies in America issued a Declaration of Independence, setting themselves up as a union separate from the parent country. These states defeated the British forces sent to put down this revolution – the first time a colony had won its independence.

Display

Display the Declaration of Independence – perhaps you could 'age' the paper with coffee. Or feature parts of it such as:
"We hold these truths to be self-evident, that all men are created equal, that they are endowed by their Creator with certain unalienable Rights, that among these are Life, Liberty, and the pursuit of Happiness."

Hang an American flag in the library entrance.

Have a pile of stuff that kids use regularly that is made in the USA.

Grab advertisements from as many American food outlets as you can: KFC, Subway, Krispy Kreme, McDonalds, Starbucks etc to display.

Hang up some American gum wrappers, coke bottles, popcorn packet etc.

Borrow some American Gridiron sports gear to display.

Activities

Have a quiz asking what the significance of the flag might be. What do the stars and the stripes represent? The following website has specific information on the flag. **www.usflag.org/history.html**

Show an episode of The Simpsons (particularly the one which has Edgar Allan Poe's The Raven as its theme).

Display some old classics by Mark Twain, Laura Ingalls Wilder, Henry James, Gary Paulsen, Louisa May Alcott, Edgar Allan Poe etc.

Further Info

For the Boston celebrations: **www.july4th.org**

For history and background:
www.history.com/content/fourthofjuly

For articles & statistics see Essential Articles & Fact File: carelpress.com/quicksearch
QuickSearch: USA

Reading list - Back in the USA

Anderson, M.T. .. .. The pox party

Anderson, Laurie Halse .. .. .. Prom

Brooks, Geraldine .. .. March

DiCamillo, Kate. .. .. Because of Winn-Dixie

Donnelly, Jennifer .. .. A gathering light

Elliott, L.M. .. .. Annie between the States

Hendry, Frances Mary .. .. .. Chains

Hesse, Karen. .. .. Out of the dust

Hiassen, Carl. .. .. Hoot

Landman, Tanya .. .. Apache

Larson, Kirby. .. .. Hattie Big Sky

Lasky, Kathryn .. .. A voice of her own: the diary of Clotee, Virginia, USA, 1859

Mackler, Carolyn. .. .. Guyaholic

Meyer, Stephanie . .. . Twilight (series)

Mitchell, Margaret .. .. Gone with the wind

Murdock, Catherine Gilbert .. Dairy queen

Murdock, Catherine Gilbert .. The off season

Myers, Walter Dean .. .. Shooter

Na, An . .. . A step from heaven

Paulsen, Gary. .. .. My life in dog years

Paulsen, Gary. .. .. Nightjohn

Sachar, Louis . .. . Holes

Taylor, Mildred .. .. Roll of thunder, hear my cry

Wilder, Laura Ingalls .. .. Little house on the prairie (series)

Yang, Gene Luen .. .. American born Chinese

14th July

Bastille Day

14th July is the celebration of the Storming of the Bastille in 1789 – taken as the moment when France overthrew the monarchy and became a republic. In fact it is a celebration of all things French.

Display

Hang up a French flag. Display the words "Liberté, Egalité, Fraternité!"

Make some red, white and blue rosettes to put around your display.

Find some French tourist brochures to have around.

Put up a map of Paris.

Activities

Show *Les Miserables* at lunchtime.

Sing the Marseilles or have it playing. www.youtube.com/watch?v=4K1q9Ntcr5g
Note that this lengthy version has subtitles in French and English – including some outdated sentiments (as do many national anthems).

Promote Charles Dickens' *A Tale of Two Cities*. Have some knitting on hand.
Make up an iron mask.
Show *Marie Antoinette* at lunchtime.
Have the film *A Tale of Two Cities* ready to show.

Wear a beret.

Have croissants in the morning. At lunchtime have French cheeses, French bread, French wine (an empty bottle only of course), grapes, pâté and your other favourite French gourmet treats.

Further Info

www.britannica.com/EBchecked/topic/55627/Bastille-Day

www.elysee.fr/elysee/anglais/the_symbols_of_the_republic/the_14th_of_july/the_14th_of_july.20369.html

For articles & statistics see Essential Articles & Fact File: carelpress.com/quicksearch
QuickSearch: France

Reading list - Vive la France

Bemelmans, Ludwig.. .. .. Madeline (picture book)

Breslin, Theresa .. .. The Nostradamus prophecy

Briggs, Raymond. .. .. Father Christmas goes on holidays (picture book)

Dickens, Charles.. .. .. A tale of two cities

Ellis, Deborah. .. .. A company of fools

Gardner, Sally. .. .. The red necklace

Gleitzman, Morris .. .. Doubting Thomas

Golding, Julia. .. .. Den of thieves

Guene, Faiza .. .. Just like tomorrow

Hamley, Dennis. .. .. Ellen's people

Hartnett, Sonya. .. .. The silver donkey

Hillard, Leith .. .. A giraffe for France (picture book)

Horowitz, Anthony.. .. .. Point Blanc

Horowitz, Anthony.. .. .. Three of diamonds

Hugo, Victor .. .. Les miserables

Le Vann, Kate. .. .. Two friends, one summer

Lewis, Janet .. .. The wife of Martin Guerre

Kay, Guy Gavriel .. .. Ysabel

Kimmel, Elizabeth Cody.. .. .. Lily B on the brink of Paris

Marcellino, Fred .. .. I, crocodile (picture book)

Molloy, Michael. .. .. Peter Raven under fire

Morpurgo, Michael. .. .. Waiting for Anya

Novak, Naomi. .. .. Temeraire: Black powder war

Orczy, Emmuska, Baroness.. The Scarlet Pimpernel

Poole, Josephine. .. .. Joan of Arc

Rabin, Staton . .. . Betsy and the emperor

Rees, Celia .. .. Sovay

Sauerwein, Leigh. .. .. A song for Eloise

Festival of British Archaeology   Late July to early August

Intended to be a chance to discover and explore the archaeological heritage of Britain.

Display

Set up your display area with a pick, knapsack and an explorer helmet, like Indiana Jones or Howard Carter or Hiram Bingham.

Request books from your library service about specific sites and put up a map of the world with the major sites shown (Machu Picchu, Troy, Tenochtitlan, Tutankhamen's tomb, Stonehenge etc).

Get a poster of an Indiana Jones film from the local DVD rental shop, or ask one of the art teachers or students to make one.

Activities

Show the 1930s film *The Mummy* (Boris Karloff) at lunchtime.

Watch an episode of the *Time Team* series.

Check your local museum for any activities they are doing to celebrate the Festival of British Archeology.

Further Info

For background: **festival.britarch.ac.uk**

Young Archaeologists Club: **www.britarch.ac.uk/yac/**

For records of ancient objects found by the public: **www.finds.org.uk**

For outline maps:
www.eduplace.com/ss/maps

For articles & statistics see Essential Articles & Fact File: carelpress.com/quicksearch
QuickSearch: Archaeology

Reading list - Digging around

Cole, Stephen .. .. The Aztec code

Dickinson, Peter .. .. A bone from a dry sea

Harris, M.G. .. .. Invisible city

Hoeye, Michael . .. . The sands of time

Horowitz, Anthony .. .. Evil star

Howarth, Lesley .. .. The pits

Jarman, Julia .. .. Peace weavers

Johnson, Maureen . .. . Girl at sea

Klemm, Barry . .. . The last voyage of the Albatross

Lee, Tanith .. .. Piratica

Mark, Jan . .. . Useful idiots

McSkimming, Geoffrey . .. .. Cairo Jim at the crossroads of Orpheus (and others)

McSkimming, Geoffrey .. .. .. Cairo Jim and the quest for the Quetzal Queen (and others)

Peters, Elizabeth .. .. Amelia Peabody murder mysteries

Peterson, Will . .. . Triskellion

Reilly, Matthew . .. . Seven ancient wonders

Reilly, Matthew . .. . The six sacred stones

Roberts, Katherine . .. . The Babylon game (and others)

Roberts, Katherine . .. . The mausoleum murder (and others)

Sachar, Louis . .. . Holes

Stevenson, Robert Louis .. .. Treasure Island

1st Sunday in August

Started in the USA, this is now celebrated in many countries.

Display

Hang lots of ribbons, friendship cards, pictures of friends, gifts, wrapping paper, photos of friends doing things together.

Check out a book of quotations and a thesaurus to find definitions and synonyms to make into large posters to hang around the school.

International Friendship Day

Activities

Ask students to post messages to their friends. Messages could be posted around the display.

Ask students to post messages of friendship found in some of the books they have read – these could be straight from the text or imaginary messages from one friend to another – Tom Sawyer to Huck Finn, for example.

Hang up a large piece of paper (wallpaper perhaps) headed 'A friend is…" and invite students to add their definitions

Show an episode of 'Friends' at lunchtime

Further Info

www.friendshipday.org

For articles & statistics see Essential Articles & Fact File: carelpress.com/quicksearch
QuickSearch: Friend

Reading list - Friendship? Yes please

Abdel-Fattah, Randa	Does my head look big in this?	
Boyne, John	The boy in the striped pyjamas	
Brashares, Ann	The sisterhood of the travelling pants	
Browne, Anthony	Little Beauty	
Buckley-Archer, Linda	Gideon the cutpurse	
Cassidy, Anne	Birthday blues	
Colfer, Eoin	Benny & Omar	
DiCamillo, Kate	Because of Winn-Dixie	
Fine, Anne	Up on cloud nine	
Gibbons, Alan	Hold on	
Jones, Diana Wynne	The Pinhoe Egg	
Kane, Kim	Pip: the story of Olive	
Laird, Elizabeth	Crusade	
Laird, Elizabeth	A little piece of ground	
Lee, Tanith	Piratica	
Lynch, Jim	The highest tide	
MacPhail, Catherine	Worse than boys	
McCaughrean, Geraldine	Tamburlaine's elephants	

Mahy, Margaret	Maddigan's Fantasia	
Mendes, Valerie	Girl in the attic	
Miller, Kirsten	Kiki Strike: Inside the shadow city	
Molloy, Michael	Peter Raven under fire	
Montgomery, L. M.	Anne of Green Gables	
Mulligan, David	Angels of Kokoda	
Naidoo, Beverley	Burn my heart	
Paver, Michelle	Wolf brother	
Philbrick, Rodman	Freak the mighty	
Pierce, Tamora	The magic in the weaving	
Rabin, Staton	Betsy and the Emperor	
Riordan, Rick	Percy Jackson and the lightning thief	
Rowling, J.K.	Harry Potter and the philosopher's stone	
Rushton, Rosie	Fall out	
Spinelli, Jerry	Eggs	
Ure, Jean	Bad Alice	
Wilson, Jacqueline	Girls in tears	
Wilson, Jacqueline	Secrets	

Hiroshima Day   6th August

Activities

Show a film of Hiroshima. There are archive films available on Google and a BBC film with excellent special effects.

To reflect the story of Sadako and the thousand paper cranes, make paper cranes at lunchtime. Hang them around the display.

Make peace signs and symbols, or have students make them, and display them at the circulation desk.

Have a map of the world with the nuclear sites made prominent. Go to **www.fas.org** and select Global Nuclear Weapons Inventories where you'll find information about nuclear weapons held around the world.

Further Info

Background and recent activities:
www.hiroshima-spirit.jp/en/index.php

The effects of nuclear weapons:
www.atomicarchive.com/Effects/index.shtml

For opposition to nuclear weapons:
www.cnduk.org

How to make paper cranes:
www.monkey.org/~aidan/origami/crane/index.html
www.wikihow.com/Fold-a-Paper-Crane

For articles & statistics see Essential Articles & Fact File:
carelpress.com/quicksearch
QuickSearch: Nuclear

Reading list - Hiroshima

Hiroshima stories, the Pacific War, and life after nuclear war

Briggs, Raymond. .. .. When the wind blows (picture book)

Ching, Carolyn .. .. Pix and me

Coerr, Eleanor .. .. Mieko and the fifth treasure

Coerr, Eleanor .. .. Sadako and the thousand paper cranes

Hoban, Russell.. .. .. Riddley Walker

Horowitz, Anthony.. .. .. Skeleton Key

Lawrence, Louise .. .. Children of the dust

Levine, Karen. .. .. Hana's suitcase

MacDonald, Beverley .. .. .. Big bangs

MacLeod, Ken .. .. The execution channel

Meehan, Kieren. .. .. Night singing

O'Brien, Robert. .. .. Z for Zachariah

Swindells, Robert .. .. Brother in the land

Tames, Richard. .. .. Hiroshima: the shadow of the bomb

The date moves each year so remember to check. In 2009 and 2010 it's in August and September, in 2011 it's in August and in 2012 it's in July.

Eid ul-Fitr marks the end of Ramadan, the month of daytime fasting. Ramadan in the ninth month of the Islamic calender which is based on twelve lunar months each beginning and ending with the crescent moon. See website in 'further info' for more information on the Islamic calendar.

Display

Display pictures of the New Moon and families doing things together.

Display pictures of Muslim mosques, sacred places, Muslim customs and clothing.

Display a map of the world with Muslim populations highlighted.

Display statistics about the Muslim world (how many, distribution, lifestyle).

Activities

Is there a parent or member of staff who could help run a calligraphy workshop at lunchtime? Use calligraphy for signs around the library.

Celebrate with food. **festivals.iloveindia.com/id-ul-fitr/** Click onto recipes on the left hand side.

The festival promotes self-sacrifice and thinking of others with people giving to the poor so could be combined with charity events.

Card giving, presents, new clothes and sweets for the children are exchanged on this day. Make Eid cards at lunchtime and display them around the library

Further Info

For background:
festivals.iloveindia.com/id-ul-fitr/index.html
www.bbc.co.uk/religion/religions/islam/holydays/eidulfitr.shtml
www.islamicity.com/ramadan/Eid_default.shtml
islam.about.com/od/ramadan/f/eid_fitr.htm

For help with calligraphy:
www.al-bab.com/arab/visual/calligraphy.htm
members.tripod.com/~theone01/Calligraphy/calligraphy.htm

For ideas for cards – this commercial site offers free cards: **www.eidwishes.com**

For an Islamic calendar (and conversion between Islamic and Gregorian dates):
www.islamicfinder.org/Hcal/hdate_pre.php

For outline maps:
www.eduplace.com/ss/maps

For articles & statistics see Essential Articles & Fact File:
carelpress.com/quicksearch
QuickSearch: Islam

Back to school

Display

Hang up welcome banners.

Display ways the library can help its students.
- positive rules.
- photos of the library staff with what they do.
- lists of things available from the library
- books that are set in a school (see booklist).

Display photos of schools around the world, especially your sister school or a school in a third world country your school is supporting.

Display old books and materials from the past and perhaps find an old desk, an old computer or old typewriter or card box or Microfiche reader.

Display an old uniform, old school rules.

Activities

Get some brightly coloured postcards and ask Year 6 transition pupils to write on their favourite reads. Display them on varying lengths of string from the ceiling. This is very effective for attracting them back into the library when they start in Year 7 as they want to find their postcard.

For Year 7 Inductions: always do an activity with an end product to display on your walls. It could be a photo of each Year 7 with a note saying what they want to be when they leave school.

Further Info

For articles & statistics see Essential Articles & Fact File: carelpress.com/quicksearch
QuickSearch: School

Reading list - Welcome Back

Abdel-Fattah, Randa	Ten things I hate about me
Ahlberg, Allan	The boyhood of Burglar Bill
Blazon, Nina	Pact of wolves
Bradman, Tony ed	My kind of school
Breslin, Theresa	Whispers in the graveyard
Colfer, Eoin	Half Moon investigations
Dhami, Narinder	Superstar Babes
Fine, Anne	Up on cloud nine
Gray, Keith	The chain
Green, John	Looking for Alaska
Hopkins, Cathy	Starting over
Ishiguro, Kazuo	Never let me go
Johnson, Pete	Liar
Johnson, Pete	Trust me, I'm a troublemaker
Kemp, Gene	Turbulent term of Tyke Tiler
Lott, Tim	Fearless
MacPhail, Catherine	Missing
McNish, Cliff	Angel
Mark, Jan	Heathrow nights
Marchetta, Melina	On the Jellicoe Road
Moriarty, Jaclyn	Finding Cassie crazy
Rose, Malcolm	Kiss of death
Rosoff, Meg	What I was
Sherman, Alexie	The absolutely true diary of a part-time Indian
Snicket, Lemony	The austere academy
Strong, Jeremy	Chicken school
Walden, Mark	H.I.V.E.: Higher Institute of Villainous Education
Weatherly, Lee	Kat got your tongue
Wilson, Jacqueline	Girls in love
Wilson, Jacqueline	Love lessons
Wright, Rachel	You've got blackmail
Zephaniah, Benjamin	Teacher's dead

Display

List all the books Dahl has written (see his website). Display as many as you can.

Display a large picture of Roald Dahl in your library entrance or foyer. Roald Dahl was more than just an author, list all his other achievements too. Have a notice board containing future events about Roald Dahl and productions of his books can be found on his official website.

The website also contains a video that can be downloaded to watch and an audio interview. Make them available for your students.

Display all the information you can find in the newspapers celebrating this author.

Activities

Have a competition for your students about how many books he has written and whether they can name them all.

Show a film of one of his books at lunchtime.

Put up a map of the United Kingdom and pinpoint where he was born and places he lived.

Have a competition looking for the oldest copy of a Roald Dahl book in the school community. Some people may like to search some second hand book shops.

Quentin Blake

Quentin Blake is inextricably associated with Roald Dahl. Quentin Blake is a successful illustrator, an author in his own right and was the first Children's Laureate (1991-2001). His website www.quentinblake.com contains ideas for teachers and parents and, especially, for young illustrators.

Students may like to emulate Quentin Blake's style of illustrations and try some of their own. Run a competition for students to design their own cover for a Roald Dahl book. Display the best entries.

Enlarge and display some of Quentin Blake's illustrations. Some students may like to do this, and then colour them for display. Collect other books that Quentin Blake has illustrated and display them.

Ask students to create one of the monsters from a Roald Dahl book or perhaps they could even dress up as one!

Have a Roald Dahl Readathon at lunchtime. Fill the library with students reading Roald Dahl books. Invite your local newspaper in for a photo opportunity.

Set up a Reading Challenge in your school, to encourage students to read some of his books during the year.

Further Info

Check out the following websites for things to do, downloadable treats for students, lists of his books, and biographies:

www.roalddahl.com (Official Website)

www.roalddahlday.info

www.randomhouse.co.uk/childrens/roalddahl/day/ A good site, but a little dated.

The Children's Laureate website: **www.childrenslaureate.org.uk**

Reading List

A selection of Roald Dahl books

The BFG

Charlie and the Chocolate Factory

Charlie and the Great Glass Elevator

Dirty Beasts

Danny, the Champion of the World

The Enormous Crocodile

Esio Trot

Fantastic Mr Fox

George's Marvellous Medicine

The Giraffe and the Pelly and Me

The Gremlins

James and the Giant Peach

The Magic Finger

Matilda

The Minpins

My Uncle Oswald

Revolting Rhymes

Rhyme Stew

Sometime Never

The Twits

The Vicar of Nibbleswicke

The Witches

Talk Like a Pirate Day

Just for fun!

Display

Hang a pirate flag (skull and crossbones) on the library door and above the display of books.

Borrow a dummy head and dress it up like Captain Jack Sparrow from *Pirates of the Caribbean*.

Place a treasure chest on the floor with books spilling out. Display spades, shovels and digging tools nearby.

Investigate modern piracy. Find articles in the paper to display about modern piracy (usually around Eritrea, Somalia, Aden, Malaysia and Singapore, but sometimes in the South China Sea amongst other places).

Activities

Talk like a pirate. "Ahoy, Jim lad", "Heave ho, me hearties" etc. Help is available on the website (see further info).

Library staff could dress up in scarves, long earrings, head scarves, cutlass etc.

Show *Pirates of the Caribbean* at lunchtime.

Further Info

Visit the website **www.yarr.org.uk**

For articles & statistics see Essential Articles & Fact File: carelpress.com/quicksearch
QuickSearch: Pirates

Reading list - Heave ho, me hearties!

Barrie, J.M .. .. Peter Pan

Barry, Dave.. .. .. Peter and the shadow thieves

Catchpole, Heather .. .. It's true! pirates ate rats

Clover, Peter .. .. Dead cool

Colfer, Eoin.. .. .. The legend of Captain Crow's teeth

Golding, Julia . .. . The ship between the worlds

Harris, Robert .. .. Will Shakespeare and the pirate's fire

Lawrence, Caroline .. .. The pirates of Pompeii

Lee, Tanith .. .. Piratica

Lee, Tanith .. .. Piratica 2: Return to Parrot Island

Lee, Tanith .. .. Piratica 3: The family sea

McCaughrean, Geraldine .. .. Plundering Paradise

McCaughrean, Geraldine .. .. Peter Pan in scarlet

Meyer, L. A... .. .. Bloody Jack

Molloy, Michael. .. .. Peter Raven under fire

Mould, Chris .. .. The silver casket

Mowll, Joshua .. .. Operation Red Jericho

Nix, Garth . .. . Drowned Wednesday

Nix, Garth` .. .. One beastly beast

Oppel, Kenneth. .. .. Airborn

Oppel, Kenneth. .. .. Skybreaker

Platt, Richard . .. . Pirate diary, the journal of Jake Carpenter

Rees, Celia .. .. Pirates!

Richardson, V A. .. .. The moneylender's daughter

Stevenson, Robert Louis .. .. Treasure Island

Stewart, Paul.. .. .. Fergus Crane

Stewart, Paul.. .. .. Hugo Pepper

21st September

International Day of Peace

A day for individuals, communities, nations and governments to highlight efforts to end conflict and promote peace.

Display

Display rosemary for remembrance, doves for peace, origami crane (see page 39), red and white poppies, CND sign, rainbow flag, olive branch etc.

Note: white poppies are a symbol of the Peace Pledge Union **www.ppu.org.uk** – a pacifist group. They are controversial in some quarters because they offer a challenge to the military aspects of Remembrance Day and the red poppies.

Display quotes from people who have promoted peace and co-existence such as Gandhi, Martin Luther King. You may wish to look at the winners of the Nobel Peace Prize and display some of their achievements and stories: **nobelprize.org/nobel_prizes/peace/**

Display various peace symbols

Display 'peaceful' books – those books that promote peace by showing how children are involved in war.

Prepare a Peace Quilt. Photocopy the covers of a number of books and sew/staple them together to make a Peace Quilt to hang.

Activities

Prepare a Peace Garden. There may be a small area outside the library to fill with rosemary.

Make a Peace Pole for the library. See **www.worldpeace.org/peacepoles.html** for information.

Have John Lennon's Give peace a chance or Imagine playing quietly in the background.

Further Info

There are many websites which give information about this important day:

www.un.org/events/peaceday (United Nations website for the International Day of Peace.)

cyberschoolbus.un.org/peaceday/2008/involved.shtml (shows what schools around the world have done to celebrate the day). (Please note you need to enter the year for the latest available information, 2009 data not available at the time of going to press.)

For peace education resources: **www.cnduk.org/index.php/information/peace-education/peace-education.html**

For peace symbols: **en.wikipedia.org/wiki/Peace_symbol#The_peace_symbol** (Peace symbols used throughout the world).

For articles & statistics see Essential Articles & Fact File: carelpress.com/quicksearch
QuickSearch: Peace

Reading list - Give peace a chance

Al-Windawi, Thura .. .. Thura's diary	**Henderson, Kathy** .. .. Lugalbanda: the boy who got caught up in a war
Briggs, Raymond .. .. The tin-pot foreign general and the old iron woman (picture book)	**Hoffman, Mary** .. .. Lines in the sand
	Hartnett, Sonya .. .. The silver donkey
Coerr, Eleanor .. .. Sadako and the thousand paper cranes	**Jarman, Julia** .. .. Peace weavers
	Laird, Elizabeth .. .. A little piece of ground
Dowd, Siobhan .. .. Bog child	**Le Guin, Ursula** . .. . Voices
Ellis, Deborah . .. . Shauzia	**Levine, Karen** . .. . Hana's suitcase
Ellis, Deborah . .. . Parvana and Parvana's journey	**McKee, David** . .. . The conquerors
	Morimoto, Junko .. .. My Hiroshima
Ellis, Deborah . .. . The heaven shop	**Morpurgo, Michael** . .. . Private Peaceful
Filipovic, Zlata .. .. Zlata's diary	**Morpurgo, Michael** . .. . The amazing story of Adolphus Tips
Foreman, Michael .. .. War and peas	
Frank, Anne . .. . The diary of Anne Frank	**Pressler, Miriam** .. .. Malka
Geras, Adele .. .. The girls in the velvet frame	**Williams, Marcia** .. .. Archie's war
Gleitzman, Morris .. .. Once	**Zenatti, Valerie** .. .. Message in a bottle

Successful Library Displays   Carel Press www.carelpress.com

World Mental Health Week

Display

Make large signs of the statistics about mental health available on the Mental Health Foundation's website.

Blue is the colour which denotes people's feelings about depression, and the colour that people associate with depression. Have lots of blue balloons, ribbons and use blue card for the signs, lists and displays.

Black Dog is the expression used by many people to symbolise depression. Make some cut-outs of a black dog, or pictures to highlight depression. Perhaps students can write on them the things that upset them.

Find pictures of famous people with a mental health issue and display them with information about their health problem (eg Van Gogh, Churchill, Beethoven, Emily Dickinson, Ernest Hemingway, F Scott Fitzgerald, Robert Louis Stevenson etc). For authors include their books.

Further Info

unitedresponse.org.uk/press/world-mental-health-day-2008.htm
Provides some learning and anti-bullying resources.

www.youngminds.org.uk (Young minds)

UK background
www.mentalhealth.org.uk/campaigns/wmhd/

The founding organisation **www.wfmh.org**

UK campaigning charity **www.mind.org.uk**

For definitions, help and advice **www.rcpsych.ac.uk**

For articles & statistics see Essential Articles & Fact File: carelpress.com/quicksearch
QuickSearch: Mental health

Reading list - Beyond Blue or Black Dog Days

Some of these books may be unsuitable for younger students.

Almond, David	My dad's a birdman
Almond, David	The savage
Brown, Susan Taylor	Hugging the rock
Cave, Patrick	Last chance
Coelho, Paulo	Veronika decides to die
Cormier, Robert	I am the cheese
Cunningham, Michael	The hours
Davies, Julian	The beholder
Dessen, Sarah	Just listen
Durant, Alan	Blood
Eley, Beverley	The book of David
Ellis, Ann Dee	This is what I did
Fine, Anne	Up on cloud nine
Fowles, John	The collector
Frame, Janet	An angel at my table
Frank, E.R.	America is me
Hartnett, Sonya	Wilful blue
Hartnett, Sonya	Surrender
Hornby, Nick	A long way down
Katzenbach, John	The analyst
Kaysen, Susanna	Girl, interrupted
Kelly, Tom	The thing with Finn
Kendal, Penny	Can you hear me?
Kennen, Ally	Beast
Kenrick, Joanna	Red tears
Kesey, Ken	One flew over the cuckoo's nest
Keyes, Daniel	Flowers for Algernon
Klein, Rachel	The moth diaries
McCormick, Patricia	Cut
McGahan, Andrew	1988
McNish, Cliff	Angel
Marchetta, Melina	Saving Francesca
Mayfield, Sue	Blue
Miller, Andrew	Optimists
Morpurgo, Michael	Alone on a wide wide sea
Pielichaty, Helena	Jade's story
Plath, Sylvia	The bell jar
Prue, Sally	The devil's toenail
Richardson, Nigel	The wrong hands
Rees, Gwyneth	My mum's from planet Pluto
Rosoff, Meg	Just in case
Rowling, J.K.	Harry Potter and the prisoner of Azkaban
Sones, Sonya	Stop pretending
Suzuma, Tabitha	From where I stand
Suzuma, Tabitha	A note of madness
Valentine, Jenny	Broken soup
Waterhouse, Lynda	Cut off
Weeks, Sarah	So b. it
Werlin, Nancy	The rules of survival
Westall, Robert	Gulf
Wilson, Jacqueline	The illustrated mum

Display

List all the euphemisms for growing old or being old.

Have pictures of famous older people on the spinner with the books.

Find some pictures of older women/men modelling clothes.

Find some clothing for older people from a Charity shop. These could include hats, gloves, scarves, glasses, shopping trolley, walking stick etc to display.

Display information about The University of the Third Age. www.u3a.org.uk

Set up a display around the book, The Granny Project by Anne Fine. Set up the display as if in her kitchen, with all the old equipment. Ask staff and students to lend you some of their old gear, or search a secondhand shop for bits and pieces (old kettle, old crockery, old stove, washing machine, broom etc).

Further Info

www.hrea.org/index.php?doc_id=869

www.theelders.org

www.tokyotopia.com/respect-for-the-aged-day.html

For UK activities: campaigns.direct.gov.uk/fulloflife

You could also include information about grandparents from www.ageconcern.org.uk by searching for grandparents.

For articles & statistics see Essential Articles & Fact File: carelpress.com/quicksearch
QuickSearch: Old age

Reading list - Keep on raging - to stop the ageing

Bawden, Nina. .. .. Off the road

Bondoux, Anne-Laure .. .. The killer's tears

Creech, Sharon . .. . Heartbeat

Creech, Sharon . .. . Ruby Holler

Dahl, Roald.. .. .. Charlie and the great
glass elevator

Fine, Anne .. .. The granny project

Gibbons, Alan. .. .. The edge

Giff, Patricia Reilly .. .. Pictures of Hollis Woods

Hartnett, Sonya. .. .. The ghost's child

Henkes, Kevin .. .. Olive's ocean

Jones, Diana Wynne.. .. .. Howl's moving castle

Lowry, Lois .. .. The giver

Mahy, Margaret. .. .. Memory

Malley, Gemma . .. . The Declaration

McKay, Hilary . .. . The exiles at home

Morpurgo, Michael . .. . The best Christmas
present in the world

Robinson, Marilynne . .. . Gilead

World Animal Day

Display

Build a display around animal pictures. Ask students to make a collage of animal pictures from newspapers and magazines.

Ask students to bring in photos of their pets to display.

Display information about local zoos, vets, animal shelters, pet shops, animal rescue etc.

Display all your animal books. During the week, rotate the books, have pets one day, wild animals another, animals from different continents on one day, animals at risk on another day.

Ask students to display their toy animals. Make sure they are labelled and secure.

Find some products to display that proudly promise, "No animal testing". Some products, particularly beauty products, have a rabbit logo to show that no animals were used in the testing of this product.
For products & companies which do not use animal testing www.uncaged.co.uk/crueltyfree.htm

Find out what animals are at risk in your locality. Display pictures of them and information about the organisations that are trying to help them survive. The websites in further info could help you with this.

There are an amazing number of picture books that can be displayed. Ask your local children's library if you can borrow some for the week.

Further Info

www.worldanimalday.org.uk On the left hand side of this home page, click onto Teachers' pages, and you will find "Why celebrate World Animal Day" amongst other things.

On endangered species worldwide: www.worldwildlife.org/species/

For UK species: ptes.org

Animal testing:

en.wikipedia.org/wiki/Animal_experiments (Wikipedia website about animal testing).

www.stopanimaltests.com (Stop Animal Tests website is confrontational and may be distressing for some students)

Fund for the Replacement of Animals in Medical Experiments: www.frame.org.uk

Please see Key Organisations (Carel Press) for addresses of many more organisations concerned with animals.

For articles & statistics see Essential Articles & Fact File: carelpress.com/quicksearch
QuickSearch: Animal, animal rights

Reading list - Animals fighting back

Adamson, Joy .. .. Born free	**London, Jack** . .. . Call of the wild
Adams, Richard .. .. Plague dogs	**London, Jack** . .. . White fang
Burnford, Sheila .. .. The incredible journey	Matthews, L.S. .. .. After the flood
Browne, Anthony . .. . Willy the wimp	**Morpurgo, Michael** . .. . The dancing bear
Burgess, Melvin .. .. Tiger, tiger	**Morpurgo, Michael** . .. . Kaspar, prince of cats
Dickinson, Peter .. .. Eva	**Oppel, Kenneth** . .. . Dusk
Gallico, Paul .. .. The snow goose	**Oppel, Kenneth** . .. . Silverwing
Hale, Shannon .. .. The goose girl	**Paulsen, Gary** . .. . Dogsong
Hobb, Robin .. .. Fool's fate	**Paulsen, Gary** . .. . My life in dog years
Ihimaera, Witi . .. . Whale rider	**Peyton, K.M.** .. .. Minna's quest
Jacques, Brian .. .. High Rhulain, a tale of Redwall	**Thompson, Colin** . .. . The staircase cat (picture book)
Kay, Elizabeth .. .. The divide	**Thompson, Kate** .. .. The fourth horseman
King-Smith, Dick .. .. Babe	**Vaughan, Brian** .. .. Pride of Baghdad
Laird, Elizabeth . .. . Lost riders	**Westall, Robert** . .. . Blitzcat
Leonard, Elmore .. .. A coyote's in the house	**White, E.B.** .. .. Charlotte's web

Display

Have a display of the staff's favourite books.

Ask the staff beforehand to select several books that they love/loved and have them write their name on a sticker for the book/s.

Display these near the circulation desk.

Set up a competition: match the teacher and the book.

Have a competition where the students pick a book they would choose to match to a teacher.

Have a spinner full of books with positive takes on teachers, as well as some others.

Activities

Read a book about teachers.

Find some books where teachers are depicted negatively. Many of Enid Blyton's older novels and other authors from the 1950s -1970s show teachers as idiots, readily duped by students.

Further Info

www.ei-ie.org/worldteachersday
For a look at education around the world – including world teachers' day **portal.unesco.org/education**

For some general information (and jokes)
www.teacher-appreciation.info/Teachers_Day/World_Teachers_Day/

For articles & statistics see Essential Articles & Fact File:
carelpress.com/quicksearch
QuickSearch: Education

Reading list - If you can read this, thank a teacher

Bennett, Alan .. .. The history boys

Braithwaite, E.R. .. .. To Sir with love

Creech, Sharon . .. . Love that dog

Ellis, Deborah. .. .. Parvana

Jones, Lloyd .. .. Mister Pip

L'Engle, Madeline .. .. A wind in the door

Rees, Gwyneth.. .. .. My mum's from planet Pluto

Rowling, J.K. .. .. Harry Potter (series)

Van Essen, Susanna .. .. A trick of the light

Van de Ruit, John. .. .. Spud

Wilson, Jacqueline . .. . Love lessons

Zephaniah, Benjamin .. .. .. Teacher's dead

Diwalis or Deepawail, means the coming of the light, or the triumph of good over evil. It is popularly known as the Festival of Light. Many people wear new clothes on the first day of Diwali, and new account books are begun.

Display

Make paper lanterns to have strung around the library.

Is there a parent in your community who would come in and show students how to make traditional door hangings or floor patterns. Invite them in to share their expertise at lunchtime or during a class.

Further Info

BBC information about Diwali:
www.bbc.co.uk/religion/religions/hinduism/holydays/diwali.shtml

Diwali for kids with lots of things to do, recipes for kids to try, cards to print and colour, door hangings and crafts:
www.activityvillage.co.uk/diwali.htm

For lots of information about Diwali, dates, culture and customs, crafts and gifts to make:
www.diwalimela.com

festivals.iloveindia.com/diwali/index.html

Reading list - Not just Bollywood

Grindley, Sally .. .. Broken glass

Finn, Mary. .. .. Anila's journey

Desai, Anita . .. . The village by the sea

Dhami, Narinder .. .. Dani's diary (and others)

Gavin, Jamila... .. .. The blood stone

Godden, Rumer. .. .. The peacock spring

Lalwani, Nikita .. .. Gifted

Kipling, Rudyard .. .. Kim

McCormick, Patricia... .. .. .. Sold

Rai, Bali . .. . (Un)arranged marriage

Staples, Suzanne Fisher .. .. Shiva's fire

Vijayaraghavan, Vineeta.. .. .. Motherland

Whelan, Gloria .. .. Homeless bird

17th October

International Day for Eradication of Poverty

Display

Put up some of the quotes about poverty from:
www.cultureofpeace.org/quotes/endpoverty-quotes.htm

Make large Make Poverty History posters to have with your display.

Have a comparable meal displayed in your library (KFC with the number of calories next to it and a bowl of rice with the number of calories).

Display pictures of families that don't have enough to eat. Be aware of the multicultural nature of your student body.

Display information about the children or families that your school body support through donating to World Vision, Oxfam etc.

Activities

Collect money to purchase a pig, goat or another animal to help alleviate poverty in a developing community.

Further Info

www.un.org/depts/dhl/poverty

For background and history:
www.un.org/esa/socdev/social/intldays/IntlDay/index.html

For ethical gifts:
www.oxfam.org.uk - go to Oxfam unwrapped
www.goodgifts.org

For articles & statistics see Essential Articles & Fact File:
carelpress.com/quicksearch
QuickSearch: Poverty

Reading list - We can end poverty

Alcott, Louisa May.. .. .. Little women

Alexie, Sherman .. .. The absolutely true diary of a part-time Indian

Andersen, Hans Christian.. .. Little match girl

Armstrong, William. .. .. Sounder

Ashworth, Andrea .. .. Once in a house on fire

Cartwright, Pauline. .. .. Finding father: the journal of Mary Brogan

Creech, Sharon. .. .. The Castle Corona

Cullen, Lyn .. .. I am Rembrandt's daughter

de Camillo, Kate .. .. The tiger rising

Dickens, Charles`. .. .. Oliver Twist

Doherty, Berlie .. .. Street child

Ellis, Deborah. .. .. Looking for X

Ellis, Deborah. .. .. Shauzia

Foreman, Michael .. .. Mia's story (picture book)

Grindley, Sally .. .. Torn pages

Hosseini, Khaled.. .. .. A thousand splendid suns

Laird, Elizabeth . .. . The garbage king

Larson, Kirby.. .. .. Hattie Big Sky

Li, Cunxin.. .. .. Mao's last dancer

Mankell, Henning. .. .. Playing with fire

McCormick, Patricia.. .. .. .. Sold

McCourt, Frank. .. .. Angela's ashes

Morpurgo, Michael . .. . Private Peaceful

Pattou, Edith .. .. North Child

Paulsen, Gary. .. .. The crossing

Pullman, Philip . .. . The tiger in the well

Stratton, Allan .. .. Chanda's secrets

Wilson, Jacqueline . .. . The Diamond girls

Wilson, Jacqueline . .. . The Bed and Breakfast Star

Display

Link up with other libraries in your area, have a display of where they are and what they offer, display their pamphlets and publicity material. Display a map of your local area, with libraries highlighted.

Encourage reading. Spinners could be crammed full of recent books classics, most loved, most read, unread, overlooked, multicultural books, future, science fiction etc.

Set up a corner to replicate a library of the past, with old, musty books, card catalogue, signs telling people to be quiet, a microfiche reader, a generic librarian with flat shoes, a bun and tweed skirt and cardigan.

Display a group of books where a library is a part of the setting (see list).

Ask your students to make a large copy of the International School Library Day logo and have it displayed in your library.

Activities

Have a readathon in your library. Invite students to join. Have a proforma for them to nominate book/s and have a place for verification. Students could get sponsors for the number of pages, book/s read as a fundraising effort.

Read aloud at lunchtimes or during the day or after school. Invite special people from the community to read to students.

Invite parents to observe a modern library, with students showing them how to use an on-line catalogue, the internet, and so on.

Publicise the article by Beverley Naidoo about the freedom books give people around the world:
Go to **www.campaignforeducation.org/bigread** and download the PDF from the top of the page, the article is on page 40.

Make the library the centre of the school. Put signs everywhere:
    "This way to the library"
    "You are only ..... away from the library"
    "Why are you here? You should be in the library."
Involve other departments in promoting the library. Languages could translate the signs into alternative languages, Maths could work out the distances and Geography could display a map etc.

Further Info

Check out the website:
www.iasl-online.org/events/isld/ (click on Suggested Activities for ideas)

For articles & statistics see Essential Articles & Fact File: carelpress.com/quicksearch
QuickSearch: Reading

Reading list - Mrs Peacock, killed in the library with a rope
Cluedo

Adams, Richard .. .. Watership Down	**Pullman, Philip** .. .. Northern lights
Colfer, Eoin .. .. The legend of Spud Murphy	**Reilly, Matthew** . .. . Contest
Lessing, Doris .. .. The story of General Dann and Mara's daughter, Griot and the snow dog	**Sansom, Ian** .. .. The case of the missing books
	Sansom, Ian .. .. Mr Dixon disappears
Mahy, Margaret. .. .. The changeover	**Stewart, Paul.** .. .. Vox
Pearce, Philippa .. .. Tom's midnight garden	**Stewart, Paul.** .. .. The last of the sky pirates
Peet, Mal .. .. Tamar	**Stewart, Paul.** .. .. The curse of the gloamglozer
Pratchett, Terry . .. . The amazing Maurice and his educated parents	**Westall, Robert** . .. . The scarecrows

31st October

All Hallows Eve is celebrated in many countries around the world. Its name is literally 'the evening before All Hallows' – that is before the feast of All Saints on November 1st. Hallow = holy as in 'hallowed ground'

Display

Display a carved pumpkin on the circulation desk.

Hang up a black witch's costume.

Have a few broomsticks out and about.

Display black cut-outs of bats, frogs, lizards, toads and witches.

Get a web from a costume shop and stretch it across the ceiling. Hang spiders and creepy things from it.

Hang black curtains around the entrance doorway.

Obtain some picture books about vampires from a primary school library.

Read them to your kids at lunchtime, or have them on display.

The website below has a template for a ghost and a pumpkin for Halloween:
www.usmint.gov/Kids/campCoin/halloween_ghostPumpkin.pdf

Activities

Keep the lights low in the library for a day or so.

Have the staff dress in black.

Have a book amnesty. Have some 'false teeth' sweets in a jar at the checkout and reward those who return books long overdue.

Encourage classes to write their own picture book about vampires.

Trick or Treat?
What is the origin of Trick or Treat?
Where is it celebrated through the world?
Hang up some costumes used by Trick or Treaters.
Hand out some lollies that Trick or Treaters would be offered.
Write a story about kids going Trick or Treating.
What are some of the problems associated with this practice?

Further Info

www.allhallowseve.com

For a detailed, erudite history
www.bbc.co.uk/religion/religions/christianity/holydays/halloween.shtml

For a less academic history and activities
www.britishcouncil.org/kids-topics-halloween.htm

Trick or treat? Meaning and origin:
www.phrases.org.uk/meanings/trick-or-treat.html

Advice to trick or treaters:
www.essex.police.uk/offbeat/o_hw_01.php

For articles & statistics see Essential Articles & Fact File:
carelpress.com/quicksearch
QuickSearch: Halloween, superstition

Hallowe'en (All Hallows Eve)

Reading list - Trick or Treat?

Anderson, M.T.	Thirsty
Blacker, Terence	Ms Wiz loves Dracula
Clare, Cassandra	City of bones
Cornish, D.M.	Monster blood tattoo (trilogy)
De La Cruz, Melissa	Blue bloods
De La Cruz, Melissa	Masquerade
Edwards, Luke	Ock Von Fiend
Gray, Keith	Before night falls
Gibbons, Alan	Vampyr Legion
Knox, Elizabeth	Daylight
Landy, Derek	Playing with fire (Skulduggery Pleasant)
Landy, Derek	Skulduggery Pleasant
McKinley, Robin	Sunshine (mature)
Marillier, Juliet	Wildwood dancing
Marr, Melissa	Ink exchange
Marr, Melissa	Wicked lovely
Mead, Richelle	Frostbite
Mead, Richelle	Vampire academy
Meyer, Stephenie	Twilight (series)
Pierce, Meredith Ann	The dark angel
Pierce, Meredith Ann	A gathering of gargoyles
Pike, Christopher	The last vampire (series)
Pratchett, Terry	Carpe jugulum
Pratchett, Terry	The truth
Rees, Celia	Blood sinister
Rees, Celia	City of shadows
Rees, Celia	Witch child
Sedgwick, Marcus	The dark flight down
Sedgwick, Marcus	The book of dead days
Sedgwick, Marcus	My swordhand is singing
Shan, Darren	Cirque du Freak
Stine, R.L.	Dangerous girls
Stoker, Bram	Dracula
Striker, Lee	Revenge of the vampire librarian
Sussex, Lucy	The revognase
Swindells, Robert	Room 13
Westerfeld, Scott	The last days
Westerfeld, Scott	Peeps

Children in Need: BBC Charity Appeal　　　Early November

© BBC 2007 Reg. charity no. 802052

Display

A teddy bear display is always a winner, as many children love to show off their teddy bears. If you ask the school to display their bears, then be meticulous about having each child have a name tag on their bear, have a list of who has loaned their bear to you, and be vigilant about security of the bears during the day.

Draw a timeline of when Children in Need first began to the most recent appeal. List the agencies, groups and families it has helped. Add the amounts raised each year. (NB The amount raised on the night always increases subsequently.)

Activities

Make the library the centre of fundraising activities.

Using the website: **www.bbc.co.uk/pudsey** download the mascot, Pudsey, to use as a screen saver, or for students to copy and colour and hang around the library and the school, or to have as a mobile in the library.

You can also download games for your students to play at lunchtime and a fundraising pack for your school.

Do you have a person on staff or in the parent body who can make teddy bears? Ask them if they can help a class make their own teddy bear like Pudsey. Some students may like to try and make Pudsey for themselves.

Further Info

www.bbc.co.uk/pudsey

en.wikipedia.org/wiki/Children_in_Need
Good source of information and statistics

Reading list - Children in need

Alcott, Louisa May .. .. Little women

Alexie, Sherman .. .. The absolutely true story of a part-time Indian

Ellis, Deborah .. .. Parvana and Parvana's journey

Ellis, Deborah .. .. Shauzia

Ellis, Deborah .. .. Looking for X

Ellis, Deborah .. .. Diego, run

Ellis, Deborah .. .. Diego's pride

Fine, Anne .. .. Frozen Billy

Finn, Mary .. .. Anila's journey

Foreman, Michael .. .. Mia's story

Koertge, Ron .. .. Strays

McCormick, Patricia .. .. Sold

Magorian, Michelle .. .. Goodnight Mr Tom

Mankell, Henning .. .. Playing with fire

Wilson, Jacqueline .. .. The Diamond girls

Wilson, Jacqueline .. .. The illustrated mum

Wilson, Jacqueline .. .. Cookie

5th November

Guy Fawkes Day

5th November is Guy Fawkes Day, and is celebrated in several countries around the world.

Display

Many people enjoy the celebrations but have forgotten the cause. Display the story, perhaps in episodes, round the library.

If you can, get some wooden barrels (perhaps from a garden centre), some joke bombs, hang a cavalier's hat nearby and leave a letter warning a friend to avoid parliament on 5th November.

Hang empty firecrackers, TNT models, and set up an old guy. It could look like a scarecrow.

Have explosive reads set up around the display. These could be those about the Civil War, Cromwell's time, the reign of the Stuarts or those with explosions in them.

Display some clothing from that time from your local costume hire shop.

Further Info

www.guyfawkes.me.uk

For background:
www.britannia.com/history/g-fawkes.html

For recipes and details of celebrations
www.guyfawkes.org.uk

For a simple guide to history and traditions
www.bbc.co.uk/dna/h2g2/A199488

Reading list - Explosive Reads

Brooks, Geraldine .. .. Year of wonders

Burgess, Melvin .. .. Burning Issy

Cooper, Susan .. .. King of shadows

Cross, Vince .. .. Civil War, Thomas Adamson England, 1643-1650

Defoe, Daniel.. .. .. Journal of the plague year

Doherty, Berlie .. .. Children of winter

Du Maurier, Daphne .. .. Frenchman's Creek

Du Maurier, Daphne .. .. The king's general

Ellis, Deborah. .. .. Company of fools

Gaiman, Neil .. .. Marvel 1602

Gardner, Sally. .. .. I, Coriander

Gascoigne, Russell. .. .. Rebels

Hanson, Neil .. .. The dreadful judgement: the true story of the Great Fire of London, 1666

Harris, Robert J. .. .. Will Shakespeare and the pirate's fire

Hearn, Julie. .. .. Ivy

Hearn, Julie. .. .. The merrybegot

Hooper, Mary.. .. .. At the sign of The Sugared Plum

Hooper, Mary.. .. .. Newes from the dead

Hooper, Mary.. .. .. Petals in the ashes

Mark, Jan.. .. .. Stratford boys

Montgomery, Hugh. .. .. The voyage of the Arctic Tern

Oldfield, Pamela .. .. The great plague, the diary of Alice Paynton

Pears, Ian . .. . An instance of the fingerpost

Rees, Celia .. .. Sorceress

Rees, Celia .. .. Witch child

Rose, Malcolm .. .. Kiss of death

Rowlands, Avril . .. . The Shakespeare connection

Trease, Geoffrey .. .. Curse on the sea

Tremaine, Rose . .. . Restoration

Turnbull, Ann .. .. Forged in the fire

Turnbull, Ann .. .. No shame, no fear

Walsh, Jill Paton .. .. A parcel of patterns

Wooderson, Philip .. .. The plague

Books with explosions

Brooks, Kevin. .. .. Being

Craig, Joe. .. .. Jimmy Coates (series)

Dickinson, Peter .. .. AK

Dowswell, Paul . .. . Battle fleet

Higson, Charlie . .. . Young Bond (series) (Silverfin and Blood fever are just the beginning)

Horowitz, Anthony.. .. .. Alex Rider (series)

McPhail, Catherine. .. .. Nemesis (series) (Into the Shadow and The beast within, for starters)

Morpurgo, Michael . .. . Private Peaceful

Muchamore, Robert .. .. Cherub (series) (The recruit is the start)

Remembrance Day

Celebrated world wide, this commemorates the end of World War One and is the day to remember those killed and injured in wars since.

Display

Display war books, picture books with war as a theme and non fiction war books.

Display of Peace Symbols (see International Day of Peace, page 44).

Set up a display of a soldier's uniform.

Display posters of the speeches that people made at the end of WW1 to celebrate Peace.

Activities

Make poppies at lunchtime. These websites may help:
www.awm.gov.au/education/programs/prepost/PRIM_makePoppy.pdf
www.wildlifetrust.org.uk/cheshire/poppy-make.pdf
www.dltk-holidays.com/remembrance/mfingerprint.htm

Further Info

For the poppy appeal: **www.poppy.org.uk**

For white poppies: www.ppu.org.uk
Note: white poppies are a symbol of the Peace Pledge Union **www.ppu.org.uk** – a pacifist group. They are controversial in some quarters because they offer a challenge to the military aspects of Remembrance Day and the red poppies.

For a simple introduction: **news.bbc.co.uk/cbbcnews/hi/find_out/guides/uk/remembrance_day**

This is an excellent site, constructed by an enthusiast, which we would recommend as very useful.
www.firstworldwar.com

For detailed background on the armistice and speeches:
www.firstworldwar.com/features/armistice.htm

For First world war recruitment posters:
www.firstworldwar.com/posters/uk.htm

For killed and injured in WW1:
www.firstworldwar.com/features/casualties.htm

For killed and injured in WW2 – an excellent summary
en.wikipedia.org/wiki/World_War_II_casualties

For casualties of more recent conflicts:
www.iraqbodycount.org
icasualties.org/Iraq/DeathsByCountry.aspx
icasualties.org/oef/

For articles & statistics see Essential Articles & Fact File:
carelpress.com/quicksearch
QuickSearch: War

Reading list - Remembrance Day

Blackman, Jenny . .. . Our enemy, my friend	**Morpurgo, Michael** . .. . The best Christmas present in the world
Breslin, Therese .. .. Remembrance	**Morpurgo, Michael** . .. . Private Peaceful
Chambers, Aidan . .. . Postcards from no man's land	**Morpurgo, Michael** . .. . War horse
Cooper, Patrick . .. . Wings to fly	**Newbery, Linda** . .. . The shell house
Darke, Marjorie . .. . A rose from Blighty	**Riordan, James** . .. . Match of death
Ell, Sarah .. .. When the war came home	**Riordan, James** . .. . War song
Forester, C.S. . .. . African queen	**Sedgwick, Marcus** .. .. The foreshadowing
Hamley, Dennis . .. . Ellen's people	**Whelan, Gloria** .. .. Angel on the square
Hartnett, Sonya . .. . The silver donkey	**Whelan, Gloria** .. .. The impossible journey
Jorgensen, Norman .. .. In Flanders Field	**Williams, Marcia** .. .. Archie's war
Jorgensen, Norman .. .. Jack's Island	**Winspear, Jacqueline** .. .. .. Pardonable lies: a Maisie Dobbs mystery

30th November

St Andrew's Day

St Andrew is the patron saint of Scotland, and Scots around the world celebrate their national identity on 30th November. St Andrew was said to be the brother of Saint Peter and both were among the 12 apostles. The Scottish flag shows the diagonal cross on which St Andrew was martyred.

Display

Display the St Andrew's Flag and have vases of heather around the library. As St Andrew is also the patron saint of Russia, Greece and Romania (as well as other countries), perhaps put up their flags as well.

Display information about St Andrew and why he became the patron saint of Scotland.

St Andrew gives his name to a famous golf course (as well as a university and town). Set up a golf course around the library with 18 'holes' each being a small display about Scotland, St Andrew, heather, flags, bagpipes, golf bag, golf balls, golf clubs and so on. You could make this a competition with 18 questions to research.

Display any information about Scotland, photos of Edinburgh Castle etc.

Ask a class to make a model of Nessie (Loch Ness Monster) to put up. For simple paper templates that could be adapted to make Nessie:
www.rain.org/~philfear/download-a-dinosaur.html

Ask a member of staff or parent loan some tartan (trousers, kilt, shawl) that could be displayed.

Find and display any novels about Scotland. The website below contains many authors, mainly adult:
www.booksfromscotland.com/Authors/By-Name
Joan Lingard, Theresa Breslin, John Buchan, Alistair MacLean, Catherine McPhail, John Byrne, Sir Arthur Conan Doyle and others, are all represented on the above website, some with interviews. Display books by these people along with biographical information.

Display a map of Scotland with some famous literary places marked on it (Robert Louis Stevenson wrote several novels about Scotland, for example).

Further Info

www.scotland.org/standrewsday (Official Online Gateway to Scotland)

For background
www.geo.ed.ac.uk/home/scotland/standrew.html
www.newadvent.org/cathen/01471a.htm

For Scottish background:
www.scotland.org

The Loch Ness monster – for and against
www.nessie.co.uk
skepdic.com/nessie.html

For the history of tartan (NB commercial site)
www.house-of-tartan.scotland.net/story/story.htm

For flags to colour:
www.crwflags.com/fotw/flags/cbk.html

For articles & statistics see Essential Articles & Fact File:
carelpress.com/quicksearch
QuickSearch: Scot

Reading list - Scotland the brave

Ardagh, Philip. .. .. Dubious deeds

Banks, Lynne Reid.. .. .. The dungeon

Bertagna, Julie.. .. .. Soundtrack

Breslin, Theresa .. .. Divided city

Breslin, Theresa .. .. Remembrance

Breslin, Theresa .. .. Saskia's journey

Cave, Patrick.. .. .. Sharp north

Cooper, Susan .. .. The boggart

Doherty, Berlie .. .. Daughter of the sea

Evans, Ann .. .. The beast

Godden, Rumer. .. .. The dragon of Og

Henderson, J.A. .. .. Crash

Higson, Charlie . .. . Silverfin

Horowitz, Anthony.. .. .. Three of diamonds

Mayfield, Sue . .. . Voices

McPhail, Catherine . .. . Dark waters

Morpurgo, Michael . .. . The last wolf

Pearce, Philippa .. .. The little gentleman

Shakespeare, William .. .. Macbeth
(Shortened version available from Carel Press, part of the Shorter Shakespeare series)

Stevenson, Robert Louis .. ... Catriona

Stevenson, Robert Louis .. ... Kidnapped

Stevenson, Robert Louis .. ... The master of Ballantrae

Sutcliff, Rosemary .. .. The mark of the horse lord

National Tree Day

Display

Have some poems about trees displayed around the library.

Borrow a tree in a pot that you could use for display. Have lots of information about trees and shrubs handy.

Display branches from different types of trees. List the things that live in trees. List the things that depend on a tree for survival.

Make a cardboard cut-out of a tree and display books hanging from its branches.

Display things made from wood. Use items that students have made from wood.

Have a large map of the world showing deforestation: List the things that have happened because of deforestation.
www.nationalgeographic.com/eye/deforestation/effect.html
Look at the carbon footprint of a tree.

Reading list - Hug a tree

Allende, Isabel .. .. Forest of the pygmies

Allende, Isabel .. .. City of the beasts

De Fombelle, Timothee .. .. .. Toby alone

Ellis, Deborah. .. .. Diego, run!

Fisher, Catherine.. .. .. Darkhenge

Freeman, Pamela. .. .. Windrider

Gleitzman, Morris .. .. Toad away

Grenfell, Gus .. .. Woodenface

Hartnett, Sonya. .. .. Forest

Kipling, Rudyard .. .. Just so stories

Le Guin, Ursula . .. . The Word for World is Forest

Nimmo, Jenny .. .. The Owl Tree

Oppel, Kenneth. .. .. Dusk

Paulsen, Gary. .. .. Ice race

Paulsen, Gary. .. .. Hatchet

Paulsen, Gary. .. .. Dogsong

Peet, Mal .. .. Keeper

Silverstein, Shel .. .. The giving tree

Tan, Shaun .. .. The red tree

Tolkien, J.R.R. .. .. The two towers

Tolkien, J.R.R. .. .. The return of the king

Wilson, Mark .. .. The last tree

Usually last week in November

What are Old Growth Forests? Display a map of the world with Old Growth Forests detailed on it, before they are all gone.

Display a tree with environmental messages pinned on it.

Make a nest from paper to highlight the plight of birds that can no longer find a suitable tree. Have some nesting boxes near the display.

Activities

List the things trees do for us. Have a long roll of paper next to your display and have students add what a tree does for them.

Have some students make a model of an Ent (from The Lord of the Rings).

Further Info

www.treecouncil.org.uk

For care: www.trees.org

For identification: www-saps.plantsci.cam.ac.uk/trees

For heritage: www.treeregister.org

www.ancient-tree.org.uk

Hanukkah is also called the Festival of Lights (also spelt Chanukah). It commemorates the Jewish victory which allowed the temple to be returned to the worship of God. This stands for both Jewish survival and religious freedom.

For specific dates visit **judaism.about.com/od/chanukah**

Display

As the festival is over eight nights, a candle is kindled for each night. Why not have a series of candles symbolizing the eight nights with the customs performed on each night, written beneath each candle. As each night proceeds and another candle is added, making a candelabrum holding the eight lights with a additional (often separate) candle to light the others. These can be candles or oil lamps, or modern electric lights.

Display any books in the library with a Jewish theme.

Display a world map, mark the counties with the largest Jewish populations.

Display information about the populations of Jewish people around the world and the counties in which they live.

Display the story of Judith. Some children may like to retell the story.

Encourage students to make their own Dreidel. Have a group of students in at lunchtime to make a Dreidel. For a template for a dreidel: **www.enchantedlearning.com/ crafts/hanukkah/dreidel/template.shtml**

Perhaps a student can make a candelabrum for the library.

Further Info

For background, activities, recipes

www.chabad.org/holidays/chanukah/default_cdo/ jewish/Hanukkah.htm

www.holidays.net/chanukah/

www.activityvillage.co.uk/hanukkah_for_kids.htm

www.ort.org/ort/edu/festivals/hanukkah/index.html

festivals.iloveindia.com/hanukkah/index.html

For Jewish population:

www.jewishtemples.org

www.jewishvirtuallibrary.org/jsource/History/ worldpop.html

How to make paper candles:

www.billybear4kids.com/holidays/hanukkah/candle/ treats.html

For outline maps:
www.eduplace.com/ss/maps

Christmas

Display

Put up a display of recommended staff holiday reading.

Display all the trimmings of Christmas, tinsel, bells, a tree, lights, baubles, stars, lots of red and green, holly, mistletoe etc. Hang stars and bells, holly and tinsel at the library door. Place lots of brightly coloured, wrapped boxes under the Christmas tree.

Have a colour that you concentrate on – red, green, silver, gold. Use this colour on the display board and around the books. Ask staff to wear the chosen colour for the week. Wear holly, mistletoe or bells as a buttonhole.

Have carols playing or an audio version of a well known book (A Christmas Carol, for example).

Pin up information about Christmas and where the customs originated.

Have a competition about what the best gift would be.

Have The Christmas Book (Dorling Kindersley) on hand. It has all sorts of ideas and projects you can try. See Nigella Lawson's book, Nigella Christmas, for food ideas to cook with classes or have in the library.

Make a book Christmas tree. Start with a base about a metre square, and build up books one on top of the other, to a tree shape – using deleted books of course!

Make a Christmas tree that has branches with books or book covers hanging from them.

Make a Christmas tree using Christmas cards, 2 dimensional, flat against a display board.

Make a huge Christmas card that will be in the doorway as the students come in.

Activities

Show the film Polar Express or the nightmare before Christmas or any other Christmas film.

Read The Night Before Christmas, by Clement Moore, to students at breaks or any other time.

Have Raymond Briggs' Father Christmas on hand for students to read, share and draw Father Christmas.

Encourage students to make a pop-up page for The Night Before Christmas, or The Jolly Christmas Postman.

Read The Jolly Christmas Postman by Janet Ahlberg.

Have student write letters to and from the Jolly Postman, and display around the library.

Have a box for donations to a Christmas cause for those who won't receive anything for Christmas. **www.operationchristmaschild.org.uk**

Read The Gift of the Magi by O. Henry and don't cry!

Ask students to supply a gift that requires no outlay of money or have them write them on cards to display to show others that Christmas does not have to be about buying.

Have a competition to write a letter to Santa. Get children to pretend that they are a famous person and ask Santa for a present, eg the Prime Minister might want everyone in work, Kylie Minogue would want every woman to have a breast examination.

Ask students to make a stained glass window for display or make a large one for the library window or entrance. Use different coloured cellophane and black card. Hangings could be A4 size, or bigger.

Further Info

For background and traditions:
www.allthingschristmas.com
www.holidays.net/christmas

The reading list can be found on the next page.

Reading list - Season's readings

Ahlberg, Allan. .. .. Chickens in the snow

Ahlberg, Janet and
Ahlberg, Allan .. ..
The jolly Christmas
postman

Armitage, Ronda.. .. .. The lighthouse keeper's
Christmas

Briggs, Raymond . .. . Father Christmas

Brown, Margaret Wise . .. . The little fir tree

Daly, Niki .. .. What's cooking, Jamela?

Daniels, Lucy.. .. .. Kitten in the cold

De Paola, Tomie .. .. Four friends at Christmas

De Paola, Tomie .. .. The clown of god

Dickens, Charles.. .. .. A Christmas carol
(Graphic novel version available from Carel Press,
part of the Classical Comics series)

Fine, Anne .. .. The same old story
every year

Fine, Anne .. .. The more the merrier

Foreman, Michael .. .. Cat in the manger

Foreman, Michael .. .. War game

Fox, Mem.. .. .. Wombat divine

Godden, Rumer. .. .. The story of Holly and Ivy

Harrison, Michael .. .. The Oxford book of
Christmas poems

Henry, O. .. .. The gift of the Magi

Hoffman, Mary .. .. An angel just like me

McCaughrean, Geraldine .. .. Wenceslas

McCaughrean, Geraldine .. .. Forever X

McCombie, Karen .. .. Angels, arguments and a
furry merry Christmas

McCourt, Frank. .. .. Angela and the baby
Jesus

McKay, Hilary . .. . Forever Rose

Pielichaty, Helena .. .. Clubbing again

Pielichaty, Helena .. .. Sammie's back

Potter, Beatrix .. .. The tailor of Gloucester

Ray, Jane.. .. .. The story of Christmas

Riordan, James. .. .. When the guns fall silent

Say, Allen.. .. .. Tree of cranes

Snicket, Lemony .. .. A lump of coal

Strong, Jeremy . .. . Invasion of the Christmas
puddings

Van Allsburg, Chris . .. . The Polar Express

Williams, Marcia .. .. Charles Dickens and
friends

Williams, Marcia .. .. The first Christmas

Wilson, Jacqueline . .. . Starring Tracy Beaker

Wojciechowski, Susan . .. . The Christmas miracle of
Jonathan Toomey

Successful Library Displays   Carel Press www.carelpress.com

Dystopian Fiction

Dystopian Fiction usually takes some aspect of modern life and extends it into the future as a nightmare world. The stories are often written as a warning.

For display and activity ideas see suggestions contained in Science Week on page 16.

For a list of dystopian movies:
snarkerati.com/movie-news/the-top-50-dystopian-movies-of-all-time

For activities/lesson plans:
artsedge.kennedy-center.org/content/2346

For articles & statistics see Essential Articles & Fact File:
carelpress.com/quicksearch
QuickSearch: Future

Reading list

Anderson, M.T. .. .. Feed

Ardagh, Philip. .. .. High in the clouds

Asimov, Isaac. .. .. I, Robot

Atwood, Margaret .. .. The handmaid's tale

Baxter, Stephen .. .. The H-Bomb girl

Beckett, Bernard . .. . Genesis

Blake, Jon. .. .. The last free cat

Bradbury, Ray .. .. Fahrenheit 451

Burgess, Anthony .. .. A clockwork orange

Burgess, Melvin .. .. Bloodtide

Carmody, Isobelle .. .. Obernewtyn

Coleman, Michael .. .. The cure

Collins, Suzanne .. .. The hunger games

Dick, Philip K.. .. .. Minority report

Dick, Philip K.. .. .. Blade runner

Dickinson, Peter .. .. Eva

Elton, Ben. .. .. Blind faith

Farmer, Nancy .. .. The house of the scorpion

Fisher, Catherine.. .. .. Incarceron

Gee, Maurice.. .. .. Salt

Gibson, William . .. . Neuromancer

Golding, William .. .. Lord of the flies

Haddix, Margaret Peterson .. Amongst the hidden

Halam, Ann.. .. .. Siberia

Hoover, H.M. .. .. Children of Morrow

Huxley, Aldous .. .. Brave new world

Ishiguro, Kazuo. .. .. Never let me go

James, P. D.. .. .. The children of men

Lowry, Lois.. .. .. The giver

Malley, Gemma . .. . The Declaration

Mark, Jan.. .. .. Riding Tycho

McCarthy, Cormac . .. . The road

Moore, Alan. .. .. V for vendetta

Ness, Patrick.. .. .. The knife of never letting go

Nix, Garth . .. . Shade's children

Orwell, George.. 1984

Orwell, George.. .. .. Animal farm

Pfeffer, Susan Beth. .. .. Life as we knew it

Philbrick, Rodman .. .. The last book in the universe

Pow, Tom.. .. .. The pack

Price, Susan .. .. Odin's voice

Reeve, Philip .. .. Mortal engines

Rosoff, Meg. .. .. How I live now

Wells, H. G.. .. .. The time machine

Westerfeld, Scott . .. . Uglies

Wyndham, John .. .. The day of the triffids

Fairy Tales

Display

Display a fairy costume, wands, tiaras, sparklers, feather boas and silvery wings.

Display some picture books of fairy tales – especially those students will have loved when younger. Would parents and staff be willing to lend old books?

Display the books that retell fairy tales for older students. Have the original fairy story next to the retelling (see the booklist).

Display all the Cinderella books (Chinese Cinderella, Pretty Woman, Bound, Persian Cinderella etc) as a group. Your book group could discuss different versions of Cinderella.

Draw large posters or cut-outs of famous fairies eg Tinkerbell.

Modern perceptions of fairies may have been shaped by Disney. Their fairy website is: **disney.go.com/fairies**

Pick different countries and find their versions of a fairy tale: **www.surlalunefairytales.com**

Activities

Ask students to make up their own retelling of a fairy tale, for example students could create a rap to tell the fairy tale and then present it.

Have a list of the seven plots and see how many fairy stories fit the plot outlines found here: **www.timesonline.co.uk/tol/news/uk/article1069369.ece**

Show the film Labyrinth – which uses and subverts fairy stories and gives a less than benign view of fairies.

For all sorts of fairy activities: **www.fairiesworld.com**

Reading list - Fairy tales retold

Black, Holly . .. . Valiant: a modern tale of faerie

Black, Holly . .. . Tithe: a modern faerie tale

Black, Holly . .. . Ironside: a modern faery's tale

Block, Francesca Lia. .. .. Rose and the beast: Fairy tales retold

Butcher, Nancy . .. . Mirror, mirror

Carter, Angela .. .. The bloody chamber (mature)

Datlow, Ellen .. .. Swan sister: fairy tales retold

French, Fiona . .. . Snow White in New York

Gardner, Sally. .. .. I, Coriander

George, Jessica Day . .. . Dragonskin slippers

Geras, Adele .. .. Pictures of the night

Geras, Adele .. .. The tower room

Geras, Adele .. .. Watching the roses

Goldman, William. .. .. The princess bride

Flinn, Alex . .. . Beastly

Hale, Shannon .. .. The book of a thousand days

Hale, Shannon .. .. The goose girl

Hale, Shannon .. .. Princess Academy

Hale, Shannon .. .. Rapunzel's revenge

Jones, Diana Wynne.. .. .. Fire and hemlock

Lanagan, Margo .. .. Tender morsels (Mature)

Leavitt, Martine. .. .. Keturah and Lord Death

Levine, Gail Carson .. .. Ella enchanted

Levine, Gail Carson .. .. Fairest

Lynn, Tracy .. .. Snow: a retelling of Snow White and the seven dwarfs

McKinley, Robin .. .. Spindle's end

McKinley, Robin .. .. Beauty

McKinley, Robin .. .. Rose daughter

McKinley, Robin .. .. Deerskin

McKinley, Robin .. .. Outlaws of Sherwood

Maguire, Gregory. .. .. Wicked: The life and times of the Wicked Witch of the West

Marillier, Juliet .. .. Daughter of the forest

Marillier, Juliet .. .. Child of the prophesy

Marillier, Juliet .. .. Wildwood Dancing

Marillier, Juliet .. .. Son of the shadows

Marr, Melissa.. .. .. Wicked lovely

Murdock, Catherine Gilbert .. Princess Ben

Napoli, Donna Jo . .. . Bound

Napoli, Donna Jo . .. . Beast

Napoli, Donna Jo . .. . Spinners

Napoli, Donna Jo . .. . Zel

Pattou, Edith .. .. North Child

Scieszka, Jon. .. .. The true story of the 3 little pigs!

Shusterman, Neal .. .. Red Rider's hood

Umansky, Kaye . .. . The stepsisters' story

Weyn, Suzanne . .. . The night dance

Willingham, Bill .. .. Fables: legends in exile

Wrede, Patricia C. .. .. Dealing with dragons

Yolen, Jane.. .. .. Briar Rose

Fantasy

Display

Find some pictures of dragons, witches, warlocks, elves, goblins, fairies etc to have suspended from the ceiling, or make large cut-outs of these to have at the doorway or by the display.

Download some drawings from a fantasy art site such as Elfwood (www.elfwood.com) and encourage students to try their hand at similar imaginative drawing (NB some drawings on the site might not be suitable for school display!)

Find old copies of classical fantasy books or pictures eg Arthurian tales, One thousand and one Arabian nights, Gawain and Beowulf to use in the display.

Display the poem, The Lady of Shallot alongside some Pre-Raphaelite pictures.

For the text of The Lady of Shallot:
www.poetry-online.org/tennyson_the_lady_of_shallot.htm
For a musical version by Loreena McKennit:
www.youtube.com/watch?v=MU_Tn-HxUL
Loreena McKennit official site:
www.quinlanroad.com

Create a different world around your display using black borders, Arthur's sword, Merlin's cloak, halo of flowers for Elaine, mirror, loom etc.

Further Info

en.wikipedia.org/wiki/Fantasy

For Arthurian legend and many others:
www.arthurian-legend.com

For Pre-Raphaelites:
www.dlc.fi/~hurmari/preraph
www.artchive.com/artchive/prb.html

Reading list - Escape reality

Almond, David .. .. Skellig

Bosch, Pseudonymous .. .. .. The name of this book is secret

Brooks, Terry .. .. Elves of Cintra (Genesis of Shanara series)

Cashore, Kristin .. .. Graceling

Coleman, Michael .. .. The hunting forest

Colfer, Eoin .. .. Artemis Fowl and the time paradox

Cooper, Susan .. .. The dark is rising

De Mari, Silvana .. .. The last elf

Fisher, Catherine .. .. Incarceron

Gaiman, Neil .. .. Coraline the graphic novel

Goodman, Alison .. .. Eon: The rise of the dragoneye

Haig, Matt .. .. Shadow Forest

Hale, Shannon .. .. Princess Academy

Hale, Shannon .. .. Rapunzel's revenge

Hearn, Lian .. .. Tales of the Otori series

Higgins, F.E. .. .. The Black Book of Secrets

Hinds, Gareth .. .. Beowulf

Jones, Diana Wynne .. .. The game

Julien, Ben .. .. Runes saga

Knox, Elizabeth .. .. Dreamhunter

Knox, Elizabeth .. .. Dreamquake

Landy, Derek .. .. Skulduggery Pleasant

Lassiter, Rhiannon .. .. Bad blood

Mahy, Margaret .. .. The magician of Hoad

Mieville, China .. .. Un Lun Dun

Meyer, Stephenie .. .. Twilight series

Nicholson, William .. .. The Noble Warriors trilogy

Paolini, Christopher .. .. Brisingr

Paver, Michelle .. .. Chronicles of Ancient Darkness series

Pratchett, Terry .. .. Nation

Pratchett, Terry .. .. Wintersmith

Price, Susan .. .. Feasting the wolf

Pullman, Philip .. .. Once upon a time in the north

Reeve, Philip .. .. Here lies Arthur

Riordan, Rick .. .. Percy Jackson and the Titan's curse

Rowling, J.K. .. .. The tales of Beedle the Bard

Sedgwick, Marcus .. .. My swordhand is singing

Smith, M.M. .. .. The servants

Stroud, Jonathan .. .. The amulet of Samarkand

Stroud, Jonathan .. .. Heroes of the valley

Thompson, Kate .. .. The new policeman

Voake, Steve .. .. Dreamwalker's child

Film of the book

Display

Set up an old projector and screen.

Find some movie posters to display. Many of the Art house cinemas have posters for sale in their foyers. The posters are great for display and are big so cover a large area. Find some posters of early film stars and pin them up.

Have some artefacts around for students to identify, such as a battered hat for Indiana Jones, a battered pair of jeans for Sisterhood of the travelling pants, and a diary for Bridget Jones.

Find some old reel to reel tape to hang from the ceiling.

Borrow an usherette uniform for display, and don't forget the torch and tickets.

What about sharing some ice creams, hot dogs and popcorn?

Make up an ice cream tray as in 1950's cinema and have loads of books on it.

Find some old fan magazines. Check the second hand shops or newer film shops for these.

Put several books by the same author together as a display. For example make a display about Alexander Dumas; find a photo, have the books, make an iron mask or have a costume from one of his books.

Put all the sci fi together as a display, then find something appropriate to promote them eg War of the worlds. Ask the students to make an alien from one of the books.

Further Info

For pictures of displays:
bpld.blogspot.com/2008/01/books-on-film-display.html
www.flickr.com/photos/libraryassistant2point0/730451828/

For a list of books and films:
www.mcpl.lib.mo.us/readers/movies/

Reading list - You've seen the movie - now read the book

Alcott, Louisa May.. .. .. Little women

Ammaniti, Niccolo .. .. I'm not scared

Asimov, Isaac. .. .. I, Robot

Austen, Jane .. .. Pride and prejudice

Babbitt, Natalie . .. . Tuck everlasting

Baldacci, David . .. . Absolute power

Berendt, John .. .. Midnight in the garden of good and evil

Binchy, Maeve .. .. Circle of friends

Bradley, James . .. . Flags of our fathers

Brashares, Ann . .. . The sisterhood of the travelling pants

Brooks, Terry.. .. .. Star Wars: The phantom menace

Brown, Dan.. .. .. The Da Vinci Code

Chevalier, Tracy .. .. Girl with a pearl earring

Clancy, Tom. .. .. The sum of all fears

Collins, Max Allan .. .. Saving Private Ryan

Cunningham, Michael .. .. .. The hours

De Bernieres, Louis .. .. Captain Corelli's Mandolin

Deaver, Jeffrey .. .. The bone collector

DiCamillo, Kate. .. .. Because of Winn-Dixie

Dick, Philip K.. .. .. Minority report

Dick, Philip K.. .. .. Blade runner

Dumas, Alexander .. .. The man in the iron mask

Dumas, Alexander .. .. The three musketeers

DuPrau, Jeanne .. .. The city of Ember

Earls, Nick .. .. 48 shades of brown

Ellroy, James.. .. .. L.A. confidential

Ellroy, James.. .. .. The Black Dahlia

Evans, Nicholas .. .. The horse whisperer

Faulks, Sebastian .. .. Charlotte Gray

Fielding, Helen .. .. Bridget Jones's diary

Fitch, Janet . .. . White oleander

Fitzgerald, F. Scott.. .. .. .. The curious case of Benjamin Button

Foden, Giles .. .. The last king of Scotland

Foreman, Anne.. .. .. Georgiana, Duchess of Devonshire

Forster, E. M... .. .. A passage to India

Forster, E. M... .. .. A room with a view

Fugard, Athol . .. . Tsotsi

Film of the book

Funke, Cornelia .... The thief lord

Golden, Arthur .... Memoirs of a geisha

Greene, Graham .... The quiet American

Grisham, John .... The firm

Groom, Winston .... Forrest Gump

Gruwell, Erin .... Freedom writers

Guevara, Ernesto .... The motorcycle diaries

Harris, Joanne .... Chocolat

Herbert, Frank .... Dune

Hiaasen, Carl .... Hoot

Highsmith, Patricia .... The talented Mr. Ripley

Hillenbrand, Laura .... Seabiscuit

Hofmann, Corinne .... The white Masai

Hornby, Nick .... High fidelity

Hornby, Nick .... About a boy

Hornby, Nick .... Fever pitch

Hosseini, Khaled .... The kite runner

Ihimaera, Witi .... Whale rider

Irving, Washington .... Sleepy hollow

Ishiguro, Kazuo .... The remains of the day

James, Henry .... Portrait of a lady

James, P. D. .... The children of men

Jones, Diana Wynne .... Howl's moving castle

Jones, James .... The thin red line

Kaysen, Susanna .... Girl, interrupted

Keneally, Thomas .... Schindler's list

King, Stephen .... The green mile

King, Stephen .... The Shawshank redemption

Klein, Robin .... Hating Alison Ashley

Kovic, Ron .... Born on the fourth of July

Krakauer, Jon .... Into the wild

Le Carre, John .... The constant gardener

Lee, Ang .... Crouching tiger, hidden dragon

Lehane, Dennis .... Mystic River

Leonard, Elmore .... Get Shorty

Leroux, Gaston .... The phantom of the opera

Levine, Gail Carson .... Ella enchanted

Lewis, C.S. .... The chronicles of Narnia

Ludlum, Robert .... The Bourne identity

McCarthy, Cormac .... No country for old men

McCourt, Frank .... Angela's ashes

McEwan, Ian .... Atonement

Meyer, Stephenie .... Twilight

Mitchell, Margaret .... Gone with the wind

Nasar, Sylvia .... A beautiful mind

O'Brian, Patrick .... Master and commander

Ondaatje, Michael .... The English patient

Orr, Wendy .... Nim's island

Paterson, Katherine .... Bridge to Terabithia

Paolini, Christopher .... Eragon

Proulx, E. Annie .... Brokeback Mountain: and other stories

Rennison, Louise .... Angus, thongs and full-frontal snogging

Rice, Ben .... Opal dream

Shelley, Mary .... Frankenstein
(Graphic novel version available from Carel Press, part of the Classical Comics series)

Snicket, Lemony .... A series of unfortunate events

Stoker, Bram .... Dracula

Suskind, Patrick .... Perfume

Swarup, Vikas .... Q and A (Slumdog millionaire)

Swofford, Anthony .... Jarhead: a soldier's story of modern war

Tolkien, J. R. R. .... The Lord of the rings trilogy

Verne, Jules .... Around the world in 80 days

Walker, Alice .... The color purple

Weisberger, Lauren .... The devil wears Prada

Wells, H. G. .... War of the worlds

Wells, Rebecca .... Divine secrets of the Ya-Ya sisterhood

Wharton, Edith .... Ethan Frome

White, E. B. .... Charlotte's web

Woods, Donald .... Cry Freedom

Ghosts

Display

Create an old fashioned ghost from a sheet and hang it near the spinner.

Dress up a dummy like Caspar the Friendly Ghost.

Find ghostly pictures to hang.

Set up a haunted house in your library (always two storied with attics, blacked out windows, chimney pots, neglected gardens etc).

Use the website below to find a list of haunted movies to list near the display:
hauntedhouses.com/indexmovies.cfm

The Tower of London and the White House are supposed to be two of the world's most haunted places. Display pictures of these places. What makes the Tower of London so ghostly? Is it the two princes in the Tower story, or the many beheadings? Make up a list of people killed there with appropriate non-fiction books giving the information nearby.

See also pages for display ideas for Hallowe'en (p52) and Be very afraid (p67).

Googling 'ghost template' will return a host of ideas.

Activities

Make black cardboard cut-outs of bats, gravestones, picket fences around graveyards, ghosts, ghouls, werewolves, living dead, zombies etc.

Play the music from Ghostbusters.

Many places now have 'ghost walks' – guided tours which point out places where horrible things have happened or spirits are said to appear. Using these sites for inspiration pupils could write of the horrors that await as you tour 'The haunted library'

Reading list - Ghost & ghouls, chills, thrills, haunting tales and the undead

Almond, David .. .. Kit's wilderness

Ashley, Bernard
Petrie, Roy (ill) .. .. Torrent!

Brassey, Richard .. .. Ghosts! The ultimate guide for ghost hunters

Breslin, Theresa .. .. Whispers in the graveyard

Cann, Kate .. .. Leaving Poppy

Chan, Queenie .. .. The dreaming. Volume 1 & 2

Clover, Andrew .. .. Dirty angels

Cooper, Susan .. .. The boggart

Dalton, Annie .. .. The rules of magic

Deary, Terry . .. . Ghost for sale

Deary, Terry . .. . The phantom and the fisherman

Delaney, Joseph .. .. The spook's apprentice (series)

Gaiman, Neil .. .. The graveyard book

Geras, Adele .. .. Other echoes

Glover, Sandra .. .. Face to face

Golden, Christopher .. .. .. Laws of nature (and others)

Greenwood, Mark .. .. Fortuyn's ghost

Halam, Ann .. .. The shadow on the stairs

Hartnett, Sonya . .. . The ghost's child

Hedges, Carol .. .. Red velvet

Hopkins, Cathy . .. . Dead dudes!

Irving, Washington .. .. Sleepy hollow

James, Henry . .. . The turn of the screw

Jenkins, A. M. .. .. Beating heart: a ghost story

Johnson, Pete .. .. Ghost trouble

Johnson, Pete .. .. Phantom fear

Kemp, Gene .. .. The haunted piccolo

Kerr, P. B. .. .. The day of the Djinn warriors

Landy, Derek .. .. Skulduggery Pleasant

Lawrence, Michael . .. . The poltergoose (and others)

Lively, Penelope .. .. The ghost of Thomas Kempe

Marrone, Amanda .. .. Uninvited

McNish, Cliff .. .. Breathe: a ghost story

Moon, Pat . .. . The ghost of Sadie Kimber

Nimmo, Jenny .. .. The Rinaldi ring

Parker, Michael . .. . Doppelganger

Priestley, Chris .. .. Uncle Montague's tales of terror

Richardson, E.E. .. .. The summoning

Sage, Angie . .. . My haunted house

Sage, Angie . .. . Physik

Shearer, Alex .. .. The great blue yonder

Singer, Nicky .. .. The innocent's story

Singleton, Sarah .. .. Century

Thomson, Pat .. .. A ghost-light in the attic

West, David . .. . Ghosts and poltergeists

Whitcomb, Laura . .. . A certain slant of light

Successful Library Displays Carel Press www.carelpress.com

Be very afraid!

Display

Hang black cut-outs of bats, webs, witches, etc.

Buy a web from a costume shop (they stretch out to an enormous size, enough to cover the ceiling of a part of the library).

Have your staff dress up as witches and warlocks for the day or week.

Have brooms, a skeleton, chains, handcuffs, spiders, creepy crawlies, Dracula teeth etc hanging around.

Make the place as dark as possible. Hang some old dark curtains behind the display.

Devise a scary tunnel into the library.

Revive The Addams Family.

Display lots of horror novels, covers of horror books.

Posters of horror movies (ask at your local DVD rental shop).

Have a mannequin dressed up as Frankenstein's Monster, Dracula or a vampire. Have cardboard cutouts of witches, warlocks, bats, zombies, etc to hang around the library.

Display some classic Gothic Horror novels and their covers. (Some of Dickens' work was influenced by Gothic Horror, and also Oscar Wilde's The picture of Dorian Gray, Dracula by Bram Stoker, The strange case of Dr Jekyll and Mr Hyde by Robert Louis Stevenson, Rebecca by Daphne du Maurier, The tell tale heart and others by Edgar Allen Poe and Frankenstein by Mary Shelly).

Create a table using the elements of the Gothic Novel explained at: **www.virtualsalt.com/gothic**
Ask students to enter the title of a scary book or film and tick off each element included.

Copy out some of the Gothic Horror poems by Edgar Allen Poe and display them.

The best horror chapter in a book is the one where a boy is Unwound, in the thrilling dystopian novel Unwind by Neil Shusterman. The chapter that describes taking apart a body to reuse his parts, from his toenails to the hair on top of his head is fascinating, scary, horrific and superbly written. Advertise material for donating body organs along with this book. It's sure to gain some readers.

Activities

Play The Simpson's episode of *The Raven* at lunchtime.

Ask the students to create a Myrmidon from Garth Nix's Shade's children (Myrmidons are described in chapter one).

Reading list - Nail biters

Agnew, Kate (Ed.) & Crossley-Holland, Kevin (foreword) ... ... Fear and trembling

Almond, David .. .. Clay

Atwater-Rhodes, Amelia. ... ... Midnight predator

Banks, Lynne Reid.. ... ... The dungeon

Becker, Tom ... ... Darkside

Blackman, Malorie.. ... ... The stuff of nightmares

Blazon, Nina ... ... Pact of wolves

Bloor, Thomas ... ... Beast beneath the skin

Bowler, Tim . ... Blood on snow

Bowler, Tim . ... Walking with the dead

Burgess, Melvin ... ... Bloodsong

Cann, Kate .. .. Possessing Rayne

Cashore, Kristin ... ... Graceling

Clare, Cassandra. ... ... City of bones

Clare, Cassandra. ... ... City of ashes

Dahl, Roald.. ... ... Kiss, kiss

De La Cruz, Melissa ... ... Masquerade: a blue bloods novel

De Maupassant, Guy . ... Selected short stories

Delaney, Joseph .. .. The spook's apprentice

Elboz, Stephen.. ... ... The house of rats

Gaiman, Neil ... ... The absolute sandman. Volume 1

Gaiman, Neil ... ... The graveyard book

Gaiman, Neil ... ... Neverwhere

Gaiman, Neil
Dave McKean (ill). ... ... Preludes and nocturnes

Gaiman, Neil III.
Grimley, Gris (ill) ... ... The dangerous alphabet

...continued on next page

Gantos, Jack .. .. The love curse of the Rumbaughs

Gibbons, Alan. .. .. Vampyr Legion

Gibbons, Alan. .. .. Scared to death

Gifford, Nick .. .. Flesh and blood

Gifford, Nick .. .. Incubus

Gifford, Nick .. .. Erased

Giles, Gail . .. . What happened to Cass McBride?

Giles, Gail . .. . Dead girls don't write letters

Golden, Christopher .. .. Prowlers

Gray, Keith .. .. Before night falls

Hartnett, Sonya. .. .. Surrender

Highsmith, Patricia . .. . Ripley

Hobby, Nathan .. .. The fur

Horowitz, Anthony .. .. Raven's Gate

Klein, Rachel .. .. The moth diaries

Lassiter, Rhiannon .. .. Bad blood

Lovecraft, H.P. .. .. The best of H.P. Lovecraft

Malley, Gemma . .. . The Declaration

Mappin, Stephyn .. .. Kiss of blood

Martinez, A. Lee .. .. Gil's all fright diner

Mazer, Norma Fox .. .. Missing girl

McNish, Cliff .. .. Breathe: a ghost story

Meyer, Stephenie . .. . Twilight

Ness, Patrick .. .. The knife of never letting go

Nix, Garth . .. . Shade's children

Nix, Garth . .. . Sabriel

Noyes, Deborah .. .. Gothic!: ten original dark tales

Orman, Lorraine .. .. Cross tides

Parker, Michael . .. . Doppelganger

Peters, Andrew Fusek .. .. .. Ed and the river of the damned

Poe, Edgar Allan .. .. Murders on the Rue Morgue and other stories

Priestley, Chris .. .. Uncle Montague's tales of terror

Rees, Celia .. .. The stone testament

Rees, Celia .. .. The wish house

Richardson, E.E. .. .. The summoning

Sedgwick, Marcus .. .. The book of dead days

Sedgwick, Marcus .. .. My swordhand is singing

Shan, Darren .. .. Cirque du Freak

Shan, Darren .. .. Lord Loss

Shelley, Mary .. .. Frankenstein

Shusterman, Neil . .. . Unwind

Singleton, Sarah .. .. Century

Stevenson, Robert Louis .. .. Dr Jekyll and Mr Hyde

Straczynski, J. Michael .. .. .. Midnight nation

Taylor, G.P. .. .. Tersias

Townsend, John .. .. The omen and the ghost

Westall, Robert . .. . The call and other stories

Westall, Robert . .. . The scarecrows

Wilde, Oscar .. .. The picture of Dorian Gray

Wooding, Chris . .. . The weavers of Saramyr

Wooding, Chris . .. . Haunting of Alaizabel Cray

Steampunk

Variously defined as "scientific romance in a bygone era" or "the intersection of technology and romance" or "finding a way to combine the past and the future" – this sub genre of speculative fiction is easier to recognise than describe.

It is often set in the past (the Victorian era is a favourite), but with technology in which modern and historical elements are combined. The term is also used for a whole movement including aesthetics and fashion. Visit Youtube and search "What is steampunk?" (You can also search Amazon for steampunk fiction.)

Display

Set up a dummy with clothing similar to that of Oliver Twist or Fagan.

Have some shawls hanging from the spinner.

Find and display a picture of Queen Victoria.

Make up an old Victorian gas light. Have an old standard lamp next to the display, and remake the top to look like a Victorian street lamp.

Enlarge some of the pictures in David Cornish's *Lamplighter* to show some steampunk engines (eg page 179 in the hard cover edition is a picture of Licurius, with his box head and gun).

If you can find *Automaton* by Gary Crew and Aaron Hill, enlarge some illustrations for the display.

Borrow some models of steam powered engines for the display.

Activities

Show *North and South* by Elizabeth Gaskell or one of the films of Charles Dickens' novels.

Ask students to design a Mek (from *The sky village*) or an alien from *The war of the worlds*. Draw the monsters from *Shade's children* (Garth Nix).

Further Info

For a comprehensive list of authors and more: **www.steampunk.com**

Reading list - Steampunk

Aiken, Joan	The wolves of Willoughby Chase (and sequels)
Ashland, Monk	The sky village (Kaimira series)
Bray, Libba	A great and terrible beauty
Bray, Libba	Rebel angels
Bray, Libba	Far sweet thing
Colfer, Eoin	Airman
Cornish, David	Foundling
Cornish, David	Lamplighter
Elboz, Stephen	A wild kind of magic
Gibson, William	The difference machine
Higgins, F.E.	The black book of secrets
Knox, Elizabeth	Dreamquake
Knox, Elizabeth	Dreamhunter
Mahy, Margaret	Maddigan's Fantasia
Nix, Garth	Abhorsen (and sequels)
Nix, Garth	Mister Monday (and sequels)
Nix, Garth	Shade's children
Novik, Naomi	His Majesty's dragon (and sequels)
Oppel, Kenneth	Airborn
Oppel, Kenneth	Skybreaker
Pratchett, Terry	Nation
Pryor, Michael	Blaze of glory (The laws of magic series)
Pullman, Philip	The ruby in the smoke
Pullman, Philip	The subtle knife
Pullman, Philip	The amber spyglass
Pullman, Philip	The shadow in the north
Pullman, Philip	The tiger in the well
Reeve, Philip	Mortal engines
Reeve, Philip	Predator's gold
Reeve, Philip	Larklight
Reeve, Philip	A darkling plain
Reeve, Philip	Infernal devices
Reeve, Philip	Starcross
Snicket, Lemony	A series of unfortunate events
Taylor, G.P.	Wormwood

General display ideas

Book shelf dividers

Use old books of a similar height and thickness to use as book shelf dividers. Cover them with bright paper and print letters or Dewey numbers on them. In the fiction area use these with lists of "Read Similar Authors" (see below).

Book covers

Use the dust covers from non fiction or fiction books to make a collage on a notice board to encourage the borrowing of those books.

"Red" anything good recently? Display books with red covers, both fiction and non-fiction.

Collect ideas from the Internet

www.carelpress.co.uk/libraryresources/Displayphotos

creativelibrarydisplays.com

www.cok.net/lit/library.php (This site contains downloadable posters for a display about vegetarianism)

schoollibrarydisplays.blogspot.com (A blog which features library displays and how to set them up)

www.flickr.com/groups/school_library_displays

Digital photo frames

Create a slideshow of book covers of new books and similar books to read

Display banners

Buy black-out curtain material from a fabric store. Find suitable pictures for the display that you are planning. Photocopy the picture onto an overhead projector sheet, enlarge the picture on the fabric and then paint it. Acrylic paint with textile medium added makes for good coverage. Select themes that you know you will use again and are important in your school environment eg. National Book Day, a dragon for a fantasy display.

Display boards

Crushed panne velvet-look material or other colourful fabrics such as flannelette provide a good backdrop for display boards. Simply pin the material to the top of the board and let it hang. Display materials can be pinned or stapled to this. Colours can be changed regularly and material replaced when it begins to fade.

First Lines

Print out first lines of popular books in a big font and post them up. Add the cover image.

If you liked ... then try these

Make up lists of "Read similar authors" and "Read similar titles" and put them around the fiction area. These can be used as bookmarks, for book dividers or as posters.

Buy plastic holders or use old books (see book shelf dividers) to make a divider in your fiction shelves. Put up lists of "Read similar authors" next to the most popular authors in your library. ReadPlus, a subscription service, at **www.readplus.co.uk** contains lists of similar authors and titles.

Alternatively you could have a "Worst book I have ever read" display.

General display ideas

Literary challenges

Post a question or a series of questions and give the students a few weeks to answer them. (Answers go in a treasure chest or a box.) It could be just for fun or there could be prizes for those who get a certain number of correct answers.

Quotes

Pin up quotes about reading around the library:

'I can't believe it! Reading and writing actually paid off!' – Matt Groening, The Simpsons.

'Reading is to the mind what exercise is to the body' – Joseph Addison

Find more at:

www.richmond.k12.va.us/readamillion/readingquotes.htm

www.readingrockets.org/books/fun/quotable

Rebus puzzles

Have these puzzles displayed for students to solve.
The following are some sites where they can be found:

kids.niehs.nih.gov/braintpics.htm (called Rebus)

fun-with-words.com/rebus_puzzles.html

Staff reading

a) Survey of staff reading
Survey the staff for their memories of a book that made an impact or one of their favourite books. Make a list of the titles or print the opening of the book and get students to guess the teacher. You could give hints with initials or subject area. These could be published on a library blog if you have one.

b) Staff photos
Take photos of staff members holding up a favourite book. Get the teachers to cover all their face up to their eyebrows. Arrange a display with the photos attached to the books and run a competition for the school community to guess who the teachers are.
Instead of using the teachers' favourite books you could use books that give clues as to who they are. Eg dinner ladies reading cookery books or the head teacher reading The Demon Headmaster.

Student reading

Take photos of children reading a favourite book. Attach the photo to the book and make a class or year level display. This will encourage students into the library to see the photographs and reserve the books.

Yearly Calendar

Many topics from the Yearly Calendar can be used at any time of the year if you don't wish to follow a calendar theme. A useful website for special days and events is:
www.earthcalendar.net

Index

Successful Library Displays   Carel Press www.carelpress.com